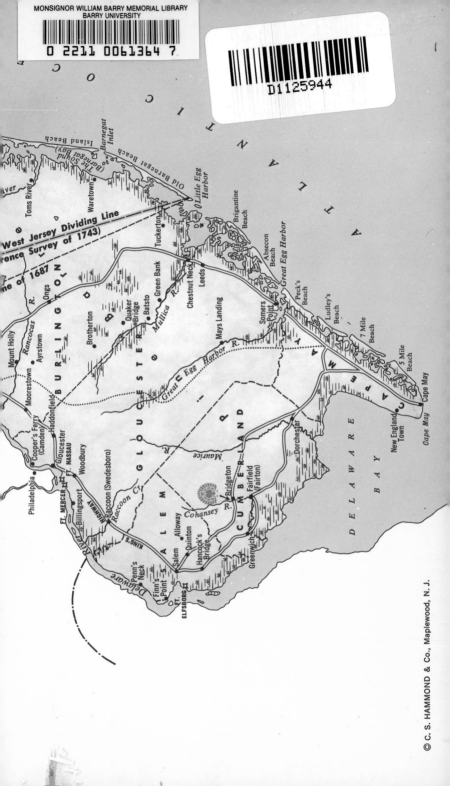

ATLANTIC OCEAN

ATLANTIC

Island Beach

Barnegat Inlet

The Sound (Barnegat Bay)

Old Barnegat Beach

Toms River

Waretown

West Jersey Dividing Line

rence Survey of 1743)

ne of 1687

Tuckerton

0 Little Egg Harbor

Brigantine Beach

Mount Holly

Raccocas R.

Ongs

Ayrstown

Brotherton

Quaker Bridge

Batsto

BURLINGTON

Green Bank

Mullica R.

Chestnut Neck

Leeds

Mays Landing

Great Egg Harbor R.

Somers Point

Absecon Beach

Great Egg Harbor

Peck's Beach

Ludley's Beach

7 Mile Beach

5 Mile Beach

Cape May

GLOUCESTER

Great Egg Harbor R.

CAPE

W

Moorestown

Cooper's Ferry (Camden)

Gloucester NASSAU

Woodbury

Haddonfield

Philadelphia

FT. MERCER

Billingsport

Raccoon (Swedesboro)

Raccoon Cr

KING'S HIGHWAY

SALEM

Maurice

R.

CUMBERLAND

Dorchester

Bridgeton

Fairfield (Fairton)

New England Town

DELAWARE BAY

Cape May

Cohansey

Alloway

Quinton

Salem

Hancock's Bridge

Greenwich

Penn's Neck

Finn's Point

Delaware R.

FT. ELFSBORG

S.

KING'S

New Jersey from

COLONY TO STATE

THE NEW JERSEY HISTORICAL SERIES
Edited by Richard M. Huber and Wheaton J. Lane

The New Jersey Historical Series

New Jersey from
COLONY TO STATE

1609-1789

RICHARD P. McCORMICK

1964

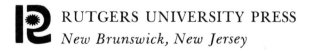

RUTGERS UNIVERSITY PRESS
New Brunswick, New Jersey

For

DONALD F. CAMERON

and

WILLIAM H. COLE

FOREWORD

Many tracks will be left by the New Jersey Tercentenary celebration, but few will be larger than those made by the New Jersey Historical Series. The Series is a monumental publishing project—the product of a remarkable collaborative effort between public and private enterprise.

New Jersey has needed a series of books about itself. The 300th anniversary of the State is a fitting time to publish such a series. It is to the credit of the State's Tercentenary Commission that this series has been created.

In an enterprise of such scope, there must be many contributors. Each of these must give considerably of himself if the enterprise is to succeed. The New Jersey Historical Series, the most ambitious publishing venture ever undertaken about a state, was conceived by a committee of Jerseymen—Julian F. Boyd, Wesley Frank Craven, John T. Cunningham, David S. Davies, and Richard P. McCormick. Not only did these men outline the need for such an historic venture; they also aided in the selection of the editors of the series.

Both jobs were well done. The volumes speak for themselves. The devoted and scholarly services of

Richard M. Huber and Wheaton J. Lane, the editors, are a part of every book in the series. The editors have been aided in their work by two fine assistants, Elizabeth Jackson Holland and Bertha DeGraw Miller.

RICHARD J. HUGHES
Governor of the
State of New Jersey

January, 1964

PREFACE

"That there is such a province as New Jersey, is certain."

With this assertion, made a dozen years after New Jersey had been established, William Penn hoped to lay to rest any spiteful rumors to the contrary. In a similarly defensive vein, he continued: "That it is reputed of those who have travelled in that country, to be wholesome of air and fruitful of soil, and capable of sea trade, is also certain; and it is not right in any to despise or dispraise it . . ." Thus early it seemed to be necessary to affirm the existence of New Jersey and to rebut and reprove hostile critics. Even today, we feel obliged to reiterate Penn's declaration.

It has frequently been noted that New Jersey has exhibited inadequate regard for its history and that its citizens have lacked the strong sense of pride in their commonwealth that characterized the inhabitants of many other states. An ardent Jerseyman, Bishop George Washington Doane gave eloquent expression to this sentiment in 1846: "We have well nigh forgotten that we have a history," he lamented. "We have almost lost the very sense of our identity. We have had no centre. We have made no rally."

In seeking to explain these attitudes, most observers have emphasized the fact that New Jersey is a small state crowded between two dominant neighbors. "We have been too well content," as Bishop Doane put it, "to lose ourselves in the broad shadows of the two great states, which stretch on either side of us. We have been too willing to become but little more than appendages to the two chief cities, which lie upon us, on the right, and on the left." Others would supplement this analysis by pointing out that the population of the state has always been remarkable both for its heterogeneity and its mobility and has, therefore, lacked a sense of unity or rootedness. Moreover, the state's economy has been unusually varied as well as heavily dependent for capital and markets on the adjacent metropolises. Whatever the reasons, New Jersey in its Tercentenary year is still engaged in the process of self-definition and self-discovery.

Hopefully, this brief volume, together with others in this series, may aid in the process. At least the familiar complaint that the people of New Jersey could not be expected to know their history because acceptable books on the subject were unavailable will no longer be justified.

It has been my assignment to present a general survey of the history of New Jersey from Hudson's voyage of discovery through the ratification of the Federal Constitution. In essence, this is the story of how a relatively small number of people of diverse national and cultural backgrounds succeeded in building an extraordinary new society in what had recently been a wilderness. The narrative continues with an account of how that new society met what it conceived to be threats to its very existence by rebelling against the mother country. And it concludes with a recital of New Jersey's role in the movement that transformed the new society into a Federal Republic, unique among the nations of the world.

Although it cannot be maintained that the experience of New Jersey precisely exemplified the whole range of the colonial experience, it is not extravagant to suggest that it affords a more representative example than, say, that of Massachusetts or Virginia. Perhaps it is because it was such an "average" colony that it has received less attention than those that exhibited rather distinctive characteristics. But for just this reason, it now merits study. Familiarity with the story of the evolution of the new society in New Jersey may afford the reader, especially if he is a Jerseyman, meaningful insights into the nature of the American epic.

Although I have sought to maintain the proper degree of scholarly objectivity in this account of colonial New Jersey, I must confess that I have written it as one who thinks of himself as a Jerseyman for others who accept the same designation. Perhaps for that reason, but for others as well, I view with admiration, and even astonishment, the remarkable achievements that were wrought here during those formative decades.

To me it remains a source of wonder that the freemen of the colony, while they were preoccupied with clearing their lands, building their homes and farms, and wresting a livelihood from the new land, could at the same time devote a portion of their energies to creating institutions of self government as well as other institutions designed to serve their religious and cultural needs. We admire these early Americans for their rugged individualism, but even more admirable was their recognition of a sense of community. They did not revert to savagery, or descend to anarchy. Instead, they rapidly built a new society.

Because so many institutions that restricted freedom or impeded opportunity were left behind them when they emigrated—hereditary aristocracies, feudal land systems, established churches, omnipotent governments—the early colonists could begin a new way of life. Because the American environment, offering an undreamed of abundance of land, held forth the promise of plenty for all, that way of life emphasized freedom and opportunity.

Despite obvious imperfections—slavery, a barbarous criminal code, limitations on the suffrage, monopolies in land—the society of colonial New Jersey probably offered as much to the common run of men as any in the world at the time. Freedom of religion, extensive participation in self-government, broad economic opportunity, the rudiments of education—very soon these came to be regarded as undeniable rights that must be safeguarded and extended at all costs. In this manner the earliest ideals of American democracy were formed, and from these beginnings New Jersey has moved in its course through three centuries.

The happiest task associated with the completion of a book is that of acknowledging the assistance of those who have made the work possible. My heaviest debt is to the Rutgers University Research Council for supporting my studies in New Jersey history and providing me with time to compose this book. I am grateful, also, to the hundreds of students who have given me their attention, and their encouragement, as I have tried to trace with them the history of their State. I am heavily obligated to the staffs of the New Jersey State Library, The New Jersey Historical Society, and the Rutgers University Library, but I must record my special indebtedness to Donald A. Sinclair of the last-named institution. Such a general work as this is based largely on the monographs of a host of scholars, some of whom I have endeavored to recognize, all too inadequately, in the Bibliographical Note. Professors Wesley Frank Craven and Julian P. Boyd, of Princeton University, Mr. Kenneth Richards, of the State Library, and the co-editors of this series—Dr. Wheaton J. Lane and Dr. Richard M. Huber—have been generous of their time and knowledge in reviewing my manuscript and saving me from many errors. The staff of the New Jersey Tercentenary Commission has been efficient and sympathetic in its efforts to facilitate the tedious business of transforming a manuscript into a book. As custom seems to decree, I reserve till last these expressions of appreciation to my wife, who filled with devotion her arduous role of amanuensis.

RICHARD P. McCORMICK

New Brunswick, New Jersey
January, 1964

TABLE OF CONTENTS

LIST OF ILLUSTRATIONS

I

THE FIRST FOUNDATIONS

THE PLANTING OF EUROPEAN CIVILIZATION in the New World, and the adaptation of that civilization to the American scene, constitutes one of the most dramatic themes of modern history. It inevitably suggests to our minds many intriguing questions. Who were these men and women who ventured across the ocean to settle in an unknown wilderness? What did they find here when they arrived? How did they go about building their homes and their society?

No simple, generalized answers can be given to these questions. In the early years of the seventeenth century many nations were simultaneously engaged in colonizing ventures along the seaboard region of the present United States. The story of each settlement was to be different from every other, depending on the nationalities involved and the environment of the particular locality. Each colony, then, can be regarded as a distinct experiment, involving peculiar combinations of ingredients. Dissimilarity rather than uniformity characterized the colonizing process.

Our concern is with the beginnings of settlement within the area that we know today as the State of New Jersey. Here, between the Hudson and the Delaware, peoples of many nationalities came together, at times in jarring conflict, but for the most part in peaceful harmony, to lay the foundations of a colony whose distinguishing mark was to be its heterogeneity. Unlike New England, where the Puritan townsman typified the whole population, or the South, where the tidewater English planter was equally predominant, New Jersey presented a picture of infinite variety. Its founders spoke many tongues, belonged to many religious denominations, practiced their arts and crafts in many different ways. Each distinctive group had its own contributions to make, and each was to leave a lasting inheritance to future generations.

THE ARRIVAL OF THE DUTCH

Jamestown, the first permanent English settlement in America, was a struggling community only two years old when, as the result of Dutch enterprise, the interest of the Old World first was focused on New Jersey. The United Netherlands was at that time in its heroic age. One of the wealthiest and culturally most advanced nations in Europe, with an extensive commerce and seemingly unbounded energies, it had already established highly profitable relations with the Far East and was about to enter the contest for wealth and territories in the New World.

In a sense, its introduction to America was an accident. In their desire to reach the East Indies by the most expeditious route, the Dutch were eager to discover a "northwest passage," through which they could reach the Orient by sailing westward across the Atlantic. It was on a voyage hopeful of achieving this vain objective that Henry Hudson gained for himself his prominent place in our history.

Hudson, a venturesome Englishman in the employ of the Dutch East India Company, sailed from Texel, Holland, on April 6, 1609, in the eighty-ton ship *Half Moon,* bound for the uncharted northern seas. With an unruly crew of some twenty men, fittingly enough representing many nationalities, he spent several months in his futile quest in the northern latitudes before he turned aside from his original plans and sailed southward. Eventually he reached the coast of Virginia, then turned north again and sailed along the coast. Each day revealed new wonders as he passed the broad mouth of the Delaware River, viewed from afar the striking prominence of the

Highlands, and on September 4 dropped anchor in the sheltered waters of Sandy Hook Bay.

In the week that followed, Hudson and his lively crew investigated the region and its native inhabitants. In all probability they were the first white men to land on the Jersey shore, although the Florentine, Giovanni da Verrazano, reportedly visited the coast in 1524. Fortunately, we have detailed, first-hand accounts of Hudson's activities, and from them we can reconstruct the excitement and the awe of the discoverer and his companions.

"This day," reported Hudson's mate shortly after the *Half Moon* came to anchor, "the people of the Country came aboard of us, seemingly very glad of our coming, and brought greene Tabacco, and gave us of it for Knives and Beads." The following day a boat ventured ashore, where the sailors received a friendly welcome from the large number of natives who had been drawn by their curiosity about the white strangers in the queer vessel. Intrigued by the Indians' deerskin dress, their yellow copper pipes, their corn bread, and their stacks of fine furs, as well as by the magnificent landscape "pleasant with Grasse and Flowers, and goodly Trees," the men were delighted with all they saw.

But within a few days, doubtless as a result of the bad behavior of the boisterous seamen, the disposition of their Indian hosts changed. When a small boat was sent out on an exploring trip around Staten Island, it was attacked by two large Indian canoes, and one man, John Coleman, was fatally wounded by an arrow. His body was brought back to the ship and later buried on Sandy Hook. Thereafter, the crew was fearful of the natives and was not unwilling to leave the area for the river to which Hudson was to give his name.

After spending three weeks exploring the great river, Hudson set his course for home, arriving in England early in November. The reports of his voyage were everywhere received with great interest. To the Dutch, who were alert to any opportunity for engaging in profitable trade, the prospect of bargaining with the Indians for the furs of which Europeans then were so fond was particularly alluring. Within the next few years several private trading voyages were evidently made to the newly discovered region, but little knowledge of them survives.

It was not until 1614, when a group of Amsterdam merchants organized the United Netherland Company, that substantial and continuing efforts were made to exploit the economy of the region. Several vessels under the commands of Captains Block, Mey, and Christiansen made intensive investigations of both the Delaware and the Hudson. During these years—the exact date is uncertain—a small trading settlement took form on Manhattan Island, and there were doubtless exploratory trips into the wilderness west of the Hudson.

A great impetus was given to the development and expansion of the Dutch foothold when the Dutch West India Company was chartered in 1621. Although the company sadly neglected its mainland colony in favor of its much more lucrative enterprises in the West Indies, it was under its auspices and government that the initial settlements both in New York and in New Jersey were established. Trade rather than colonization was the chief concern of the Company's stockholders and directors.

The center of Dutch activity, of course, was Manhattan, which was formally purchased from the Indians by Director Peter Minuit in 1626. For the first few years, the population increased very slowly; there were apparently no more than three hundred people in the Dutch province in 1629, and many of these were Walloons, Flemings, Frenchmen, Germans, and Englishmen. It was in an effort to encourage immigration that the Company in 1629 announced its patroon system, under the terms of which large land grants would be given to those who would agree to bring over colonists to settle on the tracts. This new arrangement led directly to the first permanent occupation of plantations in New Jersey.

The Land and the Natives

As the Dutch, after several years of preliminary activities in the region, prepared to extend their frontier to the west shore of the Hudson, they were already familiar with the land and its native inhabitants. Each pioneer settler, it would seem, of necessity developed an intense interest in every aspect of the new environment and evaluated everything he saw in terms of its possible utility. His own powers of observation were supplemented by those of the Indians, from whose experience the white strangers were to profit in many ways.

The new land impressed all the early immigrants with its good qualities. The climate, however, most observers agreed, was a "good deal colder in the winter than it ought to be according to the latitude," and they noted the unusual heat in summer. But on the whole they found the weather not too different from that of their native Holland, especially in its relationship to agriculture.

Coming from a country where forests were all but absent from the landscape, the Dutch explorers were constantly moved to comment on the magnificent stands of timber, especially oak, that they found here. With their practical eyes, they saw at once the uses to which these woods could be put in building ships, homes, barns, and fences. They marveled, too, at the profusion of wild fruits and berries—grapes, currants, blueberries, cherries, peaches, nuts of many kinds, and strawberries—that seemed to grow everywhere. The fact that maize (Indian corn), beans, melons, pumpkins, and even tobacco flourished under primitive Indian cultivation assured them that the wheat, flax, hemp, oats, and other familiar European plants that they hoped to introduce would do well in the new soil. Not the least interesting to them were the dozens of medicinal plants and herbs, some of whose properties were familiar to them but others of which their Indian tutors would have to make known to them.

The animals that they found in the wilderness also entered into their thoughts on the economy of the region. Here were deer in astonishing quantities, providing the Indians with much of their food and clothing. Panthers, elk, foxes, wolves, wildcats, squirrels, weasels, skunks, bears, otters, mink, raccoons, and beavers were common, and furs which were highly prized soon became an important commodity of trade. Wild fowl, especially geese and the remarkably large turkeys, increased the settlers' impression that they had indeed come to a land of plenty. Only cattle and beasts of burden were conspicuously lacking to provide all the customary elements of an agricultural economy, and cargoes of these animals —horses, cattle, sheep, and pigs—were being imported as early as 1625.

From the sea they could obtain fish with which they were familiar—cod, haddock, plaice, flounder, herring, and sole—as well as a new variety, striped bass, to which they gave the name "twelve fish." Oysters, crabs, lobsters, and other sea delicacies augmented their diet, and the oyster shells supplied them with lime which they used extensively in making mortar.

No one settling in the midst of such abundance could be said to be starting from scratch. Indeed, each pioneer was, in effect, heavily subsidized by nature, which offered him many free gifts of a kind unobtainable in Europe. Here, in the New World, where most men arrived in a condition of equality, industry and competence in the exploitation of nature's bounty were to yield rich rewards.

The physical attributes of the American scene gave general satisfaction to the pioneers; the native inhabitants, though, were not uniformly regarded as assets. With rare exceptions, the initial meetings between white explorers and aborigines were friendly, but subsequent relationships led to the growth of mutual suspicions and fears and, all too often in the case of the Dutch, to bitter hatred and hostilities. Before many years had gone by, the Dutch had come to regard the Indians as cruel by nature, hopelessly depraved, untrustworthy, slovenly, and so inclined to indolence and independence that they could not be made to work. Quite obviously such views, which grew out of the vast cultural gap that separated the two races, could hardly form a basis for either tolerance or charity.

Enough is known about the aborigines at the time of their first contacts with the Europeans to make possible some portrayal of their culture and their contributions to the success of white colonization. The Indians of this region, who called themselves Lenni Lenape, or "original people," are classified as members of the Algonkian group. Divided into three main sub-tribes—Minsi, Unami, and Unalachtigo—inhabiting respectively the northern, middle, and southern sectors of the province, they probably numbered two or three thousand when the Dutch first arrived on the scene. Their cultural standards were, of course, primitive in the eyes of Europeans, for their energies were largely engaged in a struggle for bare subsistence. They lacked such elementary tools as the wheel and had no beasts of burden to aid them in their labors.

The early explorers described the Indians as sturdy and well formed, with black hair and a complexion more yellow than copper in color. Their clothing in winter was made of the skins of deer, elk, bear, or other animals, although they were glad to exchange this garb for duffel cloth obtained in barter with the whites. The men had no beards, and their chief form of self-ornamentation consisted in dressing the scalp lock down the center of their heads with feathers and in painting their bodies and faces with bright pigments on festive occasions. The women wore skirts and tunics made of skins, dressed their hair with bear grease, and indulged in the use of red pigments on their faces and arms. Both sexes were fond of necklaces and bracelets made of beads, bear claws, or sharks' teeth.

They gained their precarious livelihood chiefly by hunting, fishing, and gathering the varieties of food that grew wild. In addition they engaged in a primitive agriculture, cultivating corn, squash, beans, and tobacco. It was in this latter occupation that the Indian women were chiefly engaged. Hunts were seasonal affairs in which the men and older boys of the tribe participated over a period of several weeks. In the summer, there were long stays at the seashore, during which fish, oysters, clams, mussels, and the like were gathered, smoked or dried, and later carried back to the village. Even today, remnants of vast shell heaps dating from these seaside excursions of the Indians are visible in the vicinity of Barnegat and Tuckerton.

The Indian villages, usually located on high ground close to a stream or river, were semipermanent collections of huts constructed of bark shingles attached to a framework of poles set in the ground and joined together with saplings. These wigwams might be either round or rectangular in shape and were occupied by a single family. Natural catastrophes, wars, or depletion of food supplies in the local area often caused the village community to abandon its established site and remove to a new location. Altogether some two thousand Indian sites have been located by archaeological investigations in New Jersey.

In the course of their movements across the state, particularly while they were journeying to and from the seashore, the Indians established well marked trails, many of which were to serve the white settlers and become elements of our later road system. One of these paths, the Minisink, started on the upper Delaware near Minisink Island, ran through Newton, Millburn, Westfield, Metuchen, crossed the Raritan below New Brunswick, and continued on through Matawan to the shore. The Burlington Trail went from Burlington on the Delaware to Cape May by way of Pemberton, Shamong, Weymouth, Mays Landing, and Tuckahoe, while the Manahawkin Trail went from Camden through Medford, Shamong, Washington, and Bass River to Tuckerton. The Cohansey, Shamong, Old Cape, and Allamatunk trails were other well defined routes of travel. The Indians also used the rivers and streams as their highways, traveling in canoes made of large sycamore, oak, chestnut, or cedar logs which were laboriously hollowed and shaped by alternately charring and hewing out the wood. Obviously the existence of these well established routes of travel facilitated the explorers' trips through the country.

The political organization of the three principal tribes was evidently quite loose. There were chieftains heading each tribe, and minor chiefs who exercised a headship over sub-groups, but their powers were limited by councils of elders, and they were apt to be superseded in their authority by war chiefs or by priests. Considerable confusion was to arise later when white authorities sought to negotiate treaties and land purchases, for it was often unclear who among the aborigines possessed the proper authority. Much of Indian life and society was regulated by religious customs, and ceremonies of various kinds served to give meaning and structure to their culture. Family ties were recognized, but marriage was not regarded as a permanent institution. Children, who remained with their mothers following any divorce, were treated indulgently and accorded more freedom than was customary among Europeans.

Although the Indians remained a group apart, resisting both enslavement and assimilation, they were in close contact with the white pioneers in many types of relationships. From them the Dutch, for example, learned much about the country by observation and conversation. They learned the characteristics of unfamiliar plants and animals, methods of hunting and fishing and the cultivating of plants. It was from the Indians that the Dutch purchased their lands, usually for trinkets, guns, or clothes of insignificant value. The fur trade, a major source of income for the colonists, was almost entirely dependent on the Indians, who bartered the pelts for objects they admired, chiefly firearms and liquor. In many ways, the natives constituted a real economic asset to the white farmers and traders.

The Indians, on the other hand, were tragically unable to profit by the adoption of the superior skills of the white man. Strongly resistant to cultural change, they were too often demoralized by their close association with Europeans, and they were devastated by diseases from which they had previously been free. Seemingly their only alternatives were to attempt to oust the intruders, which they soon found to be beyond their capacities, or to retreat to the interior. In any case, it was their fate to yield before the incomprehensible invader. By the middle of the eighteenth century only a remnant still remained, and in the early years of the following century, these few also departed. But their influence still can be seen in the hundreds of place names of Indian origin—Hackensack, Hoboken, Raritan, Matawan, Assunpink are but a few examples—and in such words as canoe, tobacco, hickory, wigwam, chipmunk, and wampum. They serve to remind us that these people were the first Americans.

The Dutch Settle in New Jersey

With this understanding of the land and the people that they found here on their arrival, we can better appreciate both the opportunities and the difficulties that confronted the men who first undertook to establish themselves on the west side of the Hudson.

It was under the enticing terms of the patroonship system that occupation of the soil of New Jersey was begun. Michael Pauw, an influential functionary of the West India Company, sought and obtained in 1630 a claim to a vast tract across from Manhattan Island which the Indians called Hobocan and an adjoining tract known as Ahismus (Horismus). Soon the region acquired the name Pavonia, after its owner. Pauw made little effort to fulfill the conditions of his patroonship by bringing in new settlers. One house was built in 1633 at Communipaw and another at Horismus, but a few years later, no additional progress having been made, Pauw was induced to relinquish his claim to the Company.

In the years that followed, several venturesome settlers and their families occupied scattered homesteads in Pavonia. For a while all went well, but early in 1643, as the result of the clumsy handling of a minor incident by the Company's resident Director, savage warfare broke out between the Dutch and the Indians, with Pavonia a principal battleground. When the conflict subsided nearly two years later, Pavonia had been devastated, and its inhabitants undertook the laborious tasks of rebuilding their homes and farms.

In the ensuing decade of peace, the strip between Hoboken and Bayonne became dotted with farms. Agriculture, lumbering, fishing, and fur trading were carried on successfully, and the future seemed promising. But in September, 1655, while Governor Stuyvesant was engaged in ousting the Swedes from the lower Delaware, another Indian war broke out and the Dutch settlements in New Jersey and Manhattan suffered heavy loss of life and property. For the second time Pavonia was left in ruins. Its inhabitants fled to Manhattan, and for several years the region remained deserted.

Not until 1658 did the settlers return to the west shore, and then they were required by the Director, Peter Stuyvesant, to concentrate their houses within a stockaded village. So it was that the Town of Bergen, the first town in New Jersey, was founded in 1660 on the heights behind Communipaw, now the heart of Jersey City. Town plots were allotted to the several families who had their farms in the outlying region. A year later the town was permitted to have its own court and local government, marking the beginnings of political institutions in New Jersey. Meanwhile, the settlement at Communipaw was consolidated and fortified and was connected with Bergen by a road. Thus by 1664, after a half-century of colonizing activity on the Hudson, the Dutch had barely succeeded in developing two small villages on the Jersey shore.

Elsewhere within the bounds of the present-day State of New Jersey, there was little activity. Fort Nassau, which had been erected in 1623 near what is now Gloucester on the Delaware, was occupied intermittently down to 1651, when it was finally abandoned. Plans for a patroonship on Cape May similarly produced nothing of permanence. In the northwestern corner of the state there was some interest in the exploitation of possible mineral resources, which resulted in the opening of the Old Mine Road from near the Delaware Water Gap to

Kingston, New York. Manhattan Island possessed so many attractions and economic advantages and the Indian menace was so real across the Hudson that the Dutch had little inducement for extending their area of settlement. Probably there were no more than two hundred white inhabitants in New Jersey when the Dutch regime came to an end.

The Swedes on the Delaware

While the Dutch were struggling to secure and maintain their hold on the valley of the Hudson, the Delaware region was the scene of poorly conceived and feebly supported colonizing activities by the Swedes. At that time at the peak of its national power and prestige, Sweden was induced to embark on this ill-fated project by certain men, among them William Usselinx and Peter Minuit, who had earlier been influential in the affairs of the Dutch West India Company. Actually, the Delaware enterprise met with little genuine enthusiasm in Sweden, for few Swedes had any desire to emigrate and European concerns largely absorbed the energies of the Swedish government.

After several false starts, the first Swedish expedition arrived in the Delaware in 1638 under the command of Minuit. A settlement was made at Fort Christina (Wilmington), and for the next several years the colony barely sustained itself. A few years later, in 1643, Fort Nya Elfsborg was built on the Jersey shore of the Delaware below Salem Creek. Its small garrison was supposed to protect Swedish interests in the fur trade against English and Dutch intrusions, but after some years it was abandoned. According to the early accounts, the soldiers found it impossible to dwell there because of the torments inflicted on them by the swarms of mosquitoes that infested the place.

Although the Dutch had asserted prior claims to the Delaware valley and had a continuing interest in the Indian trade there, they were not at first disposed to challenge the Swedish interlopers. But as the Swedes sought to extend their control up the valley as far as present-day Trenton, building forts and blockhouses along the river, the Dutch foresaw the loss of their profitable trade with the Indians of the region. After some preliminary sparring, Governor Stuyvesant led an expedition of seven ships and six hundred soldiers to the Delaware in late August, 1655, and with a minimum of fighting induced the Swedish commander to surrender Sweden's claims.

The entire Swedish colony at the time embraced fewer than four hundred people, many of whom were not Swedes but Finns or former residents of the Low Countries. After the Dutch conquest, many returned to their homelands or migrated to New York, but enough of them remained to leave a permanent impression on the lower Delaware. In subsequent years, especially after 1664, they took up lands on the east side of the river in large numbers where today such place names as Finns Point, Swedesboro, Elsinboro, and Mullica Hill commemorate the only attempt at American colonization made by the Swedish nation.

Down to the year 1664, then, despite several decades of colonizing activity by the Dutch and the Swedes in the valleys of the Hudson and the Delaware, the land between the two great rivers remained all but neglected. Except for Bergen there was no organized community of white settlers. Neither the Netherlands nor Sweden, it would seem, had the capacity or the will to undertake the planting of European civilization throughout the areas to which they laid claim. As they faltered in their inadequate efforts, other men, in New England and in England, looked covetously at the rich lands between the rivers and laid plans to wrest them from the Dutch. Paradoxically, it was not until after the Dutch flag had ceased to fly over Manhattan that the Dutch moved into New Jersey in great numbers from New York and made the valleys of the Hackensack and the Raritan more Dutch than New Amsterdam.

II

PROPRIETARY EAST JERSEY

During the half-century that the Dutch were engaging in their indecisive ventures along the Hudson, the English were demonstrating a sustained and vigorous colonizing ability both in New England and in the Chesapeake region. As the area of English settlement steadily expanded, and as Anglo-Dutch commercial rivalries approached a climax, the future of New Netherland was placed in jeopardy.

The English had never conceded the right of the Dutch or the Swedes to occupy any portion of North America. On the extremely dubious basis of the voyage of discovery made by John Cabot in 1497, they chose to regard all other nations as interlopers. This attitude was soon adopted by the energetic New Englanders, with the result that the Dutch were often made rudely aware of the precarious nature of their tenure by persistent intrusions within their domain.

Captain Thomas Yong was representative of this audacious spirit. Sailing from England in 1634 with a royal commission to explore new lands, Yong and his nephew, Robert Evelyn, ultimately entered the Delaware River and ascended it as far as Trenton. There they encountered two startled Dutch traders, whom they succeeded in persuading that the river rightfully belonged to the King. Some years after his return to England, Evelyn published the first English descriptive account of New Jersey, briefly titled *Directions for Adventurers* (1648).

In the same year that Yong began his voyage, New Jersey was included within a vast but vaguely defined region given by Charles I to Sir Edmund Plowden and his associates. Plowden, who called his grant New Albion, styled himself Earl Palatine and had visions of peopling his province with noble knights who would undertake the conversion of the mythical 23 Indian kings who dwelled there. The romantic proprietor came to America in 1642 and visited the Delaware settlements, where he evidently had little success in establishing his government. After further strange adventures he returned to England and was doubtless responsible for the publication of the fanciful *Description of the Province of New Albion,* purportedly written by "Beauchamp Plantagenet of Belvil, in New Albion."

No more was heard of Plowden's grant until 1784, when one Charles Varlo, claiming to be the successor to Plowden's rights, made his appearance in New Jersey. Soon advertisements appeared in the newspapers cautioning the good citizens of New Jersey that they must not buy any land in the State except from the rightful owner, Varlo. With this final fantastic episode, the strange history of New Albion ended.

The intrusions of Yong and Plowden were minor annoyances to the Dutch. More serious were the threats from New England and especially from the tiny but aggressive New Haven Colony. As early as 1642, a small company of some sixty settlers from New Haven established themselves below what is today the town of Salem. Although they were soon induced to depart from the region by the Swedes, they persisted in upholding their claims for several years. In 1651 and again in 1655, similar expeditions were organized to take up lands on the Delaware, but in each case circumstances intervened to prevent the realization of the project. The interest continued, and in the last years of the Dutch regime, protracted negotiations were being carried on between Governor Stuyvesant and the New Haven authorities, who endeavored to acquire lands in North Jersey for their people. Meanwhile other New England groups were urging upon the King the desirability of ousting the

Dutch from their domain. Pressures were building up that were soon to erupt and to make New Jersey a beckoning frontier for land-hungry Puritans.

Over in England, powerful forces were converging with the purpose of eliminating the Dutch salient. Charles II had returned to the throne in 1660 with meager financial resources and a host of friends whom he could reward in no better way than with grants of land in the colonies. His brother James, Duke of York, became a leader of a faction that wanted to crush Dutch commercial power. In his capacity as Lord High Admiral and as the chief promoter of the Royal African Company, which competed with the Dutch in the lucrative slave trade, the Duke was more than disposed to press for action against New Netherland.

Early in 1664 the decision was made to send a fleet to America. The House of Commons gave its support to the project. The crucial step was taken on March 12 when the King gave his brother a royal patent for the region between the Connecticut and the Delaware Rivers, and in addition for part of Maine, Long Island, Martha's Vineyard, and Nantucket Island. Later, the west bank of the Delaware was appended to this strangely assorted domain. The Duke, by this patent, was invested not only with ownership of the soil but also with full powers of governing the vast area under his control. All that remained to be done was to eliminate the Dutch.

An expeditionary force of four ships and a few hundred troops sailed from England in May to accomplish this objective. After a brief stop at Boston, the fleet arrived at New Amsterdam in mid-August. The Dutch situation was hopeless in the face of the superior British might, and Holland had to pay a price for its years of indifference and neglect. Without the firing of a shot, Governor Stuyvesant was forced to capitulate, and on September 7, 1664, New Amsterdam became New York. In the course of the succeeding few weeks, the English colors were raised over Albany, and the settlements on the Delaware were also, with some unnecessary brutality, taken over. Out of these incidents grew a general war between the English and the Dutch, but at its conclusion in 1667, the English were confirmed in their new possessions by the Treaty of Breda.

Thus it was that the English came into possession of New Jersey. Heretofore all of the colonizing ventures in America had been undertaken by individuals or by private companies. Now, for the first time, the official might of the British government had been used to conquer and found a vast proprietary colony held by the brother of the King. As affairs subsequently developed, the Dutch inhabitants were not adversely affected by the change of rulers, especially the small number in New Jersey. They retained their property and, in fact, soon were able to acquire land on more generous terms than had formerly prevailed. Moreover, English rule was to bring about a more rapid development of the region than had been possible under the Dutch.

FOUNDING THE EARLY TOWNS

Within a few years after the termination of Dutch rule, there was a large influx of people—chiefly from Long Island and New England—into Jersey. Towns were founded, land was distributed and brought under cultivation, governmental institutions were established, and a society emerged with characteristics that strongly influenced the later history of the colony. Less promising was the fact that the basis was laid for certain confusing conflicts that were to complicate the economic and political life of New Jersey for over a century.

The key to the problems that subsequently vexed the province was an accident of chronology. After the Duke of York's expedition had sailed for America, the Duke decided to part with a portion of the domain that he had not yet acquired. That is, on June 23 and 24, 1664, he conveyed to two close friends who had served the royal cause well in the years of adversity the territory we know today as New Jersey. These courtiers, Sir George Carteret and John, Lord Berkeley, were given full ownership of the soil; they also assumed that they possessed powers of government.*

The two proprietors of New Jersey were men of considerable importance in Restoration England. Both had served the royal cause valiantly during the trying years of the Civil War and the Commonwealth, Berkeley as a soldier in the field and as a close confidant of the exiled princes and Carteret as a daring seaman and commander of the last royalist stronghold, his native island of Jersey. Indeed, while Charles was in Jersey under the protection of Carteret, he manifested his gratitude, in February, 1650, by granting Sir George an island off Virginia "to be called New Jersey." Carteret sent out an expedition to colonize this first New Jersey, but his ship was captured by the Cromwellians, and the effort was abandoned. When Charles II ascended the throne, he rewarded Berkeley with appointments as master of ordnance and membership in the privy council. Carteret also was appointed to the privy council and was named treasurer of the navy and vice-chamberlain. It was doubtless with some remembrance of the previous grant of 1650 that the new province was called New Jersey.

As proprietors of New Jersey, Berkeley and Carteret hoped to receive a goodly income from their lands, although neither entertained any thoughts of taking up residence in America. Their interest was exclusively economic. Now the difficulty was that the Duke had sent to America with his expedition a governor, Colonel Richard Nicolls, who was given wide latitude in administering the Duke's possession. Because of the poor com-

---

* The status of New Jersey was not unique; there were other proprietary colonies, including Maryland, the Carolinas, and New York, and subsequently, Pennsylvania and Delaware. In each instance a grant was made to one or more individuals, conferring on them and their successors a vast territory. In broad terms, the proprietors were empowered to devise a frame of government for their domain and to appoint a governor or deputy-governor. As the owners of all the ungranted land within their jurisdiction, they were free to arrange whatever method they chose for dividing, selling, or otherwise disposing of it. In effect, the Crown entrusted to the proprietors virtually full responsibility for the development of a colony at no direct expense to the British treasury.

Sir George Carteret

A native of the island of Jersey, Sir George Carteret became the co-proprietor of New Jersey with John Lord Berkeley, on June 23-24, 1664.

munications at that time, it was many months before he learned that his royal master had disposed of New Jersey. In the meantime, Nicolls in good faith had parceled out to companies of settlers vast tracts in New Jersey. As a consequence, much confusion was to ensue over land titles.

In the same month that New Amsterdam fell, Colonel Nicolls received a request from a group of men then residing in Jamaica, Long Island, for permission to take up lands in New Jersey. These "associates," as they were to be called, had previously carried on unsuccessful negotiations with the Dutch with the same objective. Nicolls promptly gave his approval to the project, and late in October, 1664, John Bailey, Daniel Denton, and Luke Watson—on behalf of the associates—purchased from the local Indian chieftains a region that extended from the Raritan to the Passaic and ran roughly some thirty miles into the back country. For this immense tract, now one of the most populous areas of the State, the Indians received twenty fathoms of trading cloth, two coats, two guns, two kettles, ten bars of lead, twenty handfuls of powder, and four hundred fathoms of white wampum. Nicolls confirmed this action in December, and soon many families left Jamaica for the great American adventure of founding a community in the wilderness.

Following the typical New England pattern, the new settlers established themselves in a compact town, which was named Elizabethtown, presumably to honor the wife of Sir George Carteret. Each associate had his home lot and a small farm nearby. Initially no payments were made for land except for the goods paid to the Indians. Ultimately, however, it was specifically provided that an annual rent "according to the Customary rate of the Country for new Plantations" should be paid to the Duke.

Another group of prospective settlers went through a similar process and in April, 1665, received from Colonel Nicolls a confirmation of their title to the Monmouth Grant. This tract embraced a vaguely defined area a dozen miles wide running from Sandy Hook westward on the south side of Raritan Bay. The pioneers who moved into this area were chiefly Baptists from Rhode Island and Quakers from Gravesend, Long Island. The latter group, particularly, was motivated by a desire to escape from restrictions on their religious freedom. In his grant, Nicolls assured the settlers complete liberty of conscience and in addition conferred on them the unusual privilege of having their own representative assembly and their own courts. Payments of rent to the Duke were to begin after seven years. From this enterprise the two towns of Shrewsbury and Middletown developed.

While these transactions were taking place under the jurisdiction of Colonel Nicolls, Berkeley and Carteret were making their own plans in England for the province. After drawing up a "Frame of Government," they appointed Captain Philip Carteret, twenty-six-year-old cousin of Sir George, as governor and dispatched him to New Jersey. There he arrived in August, 1665, aboard the ship *Philip* with some thirty gentlemen and servants, Frenchmen and Englishmen, some of them from the Channel Islands. Elizabethtown, which he selected as his capital, had barely been established, when it assumed a heterogeneous character because of the contrast between Carteret's followers and the transplanted Puritans from Jamaica.

Carteret was well aware of the fact that Nicolls had alienated two large and valuable tracts of the proprietors' domain, but initially he seems to have accepted the situation. He himself became a shareholder in the Elizabethtown associates and participated in and confirmed the sale of the lower half of their tract to a company of New Englanders in December, 1666. Very soon the purchasers established the two towns of Woodbridge and Piscataway.

The new governor also gave his encouragement and assistance to a company of settlers from the defunct New Haven Colony who had for several years manifested an interest in removing to New Jersey. After purchasing title to their lands from the Indians, these men under the

The Arrival of Governor Carteret

Philip Carteret, a distant relation of the proprietor, landed at Elizabethtown in August, 1665, to inaugurate the proprietary regime in New Jersey.

leadership of the renowned Robert Treat were granted the area bounded by Newark Bay, the Passaic River, and the Watchung Mountains. It was their intention to establish a community on strict Puritan principles. Accordingly, they decreed that only those who were members of Congregational churches should be permitted to participate in the government of the town. The first settlers arrived in 1666, and a year later the town was given the name of Newark.

Thus within little more than two years after the Dutch surrender, the foundations were laid for six new towns: Elizabethtown, Middletown, Shrewsbury, Woodbridge, Piscataway, and Newark. In each case the settlements were carried out not by lone individuals but by groups, or associates, who laid out their homesteads within a compact area. These experienced colonists were strongly influenced by their New England background. Except for the Baptists in Piscataway and Middletown and the Quakers in Shrewsbury, they represented an extension of the Puritan influence. In time they were all to prove themselves to be stubbornly dedicated to principles of personal independence and representative self-government. Having tested the limits of self-reliance in their stern role of pioneers, they were not disposed to submit meekly to any man as their political or economic master.

In addition to these six towns, there was, of course, the Dutch village of Bergen, to which Governor Carteret granted a charter in September, 1668. There were a few isolated settlers, chiefly Dutch, on the Delaware, but there were to be no organized towns in that area for a decade. Carteret also conveyed to certain individuals large tracts between the Hackensack and Passaic rivers and smaller grants in the vicinity of Bergen. In general, though, the pattern of settlement in these early years was basically that of the compact agricultural village.

CARTERET'S GOVERNORSHIP

The early years of the proprietary regime constitute perhaps the most significant brief period in the history of New Jersey. For these were the formative years, the years when basic governmental institutions were being developed and tested, political practices were taking form, far-reaching land policies were becoming fixed, and the pattern of economic life was emerging. The course of public affairs was far from tranquil. On the contrary, the proprietary regime was an exceedingly turbulent one, disturbed and even shattered by wars, revolts, and abrupt shifts in English policy. Nevertheless, in spite of discord and instability, the several towns grew and prospered, and the new society took on a distinctive character.

The form of government of the province was determined by the two proprietors, Berkeley and Carteret. Although their legal right to assume governmental authority was far from clear, and was ultimately to be challenged successfully by the Crown, they proceeded to draw up a constitution for the province in 1665. Copied very largely from the basic charter of the Carolina Colony, in which the two courtiers were also interested, it has become known as the Concessions and Agreement of 1665. Berkeley and Carteret were essentially real estate promoters, anxious to attract settlers to their domain in order that they might derive a profitable revenue from land rents. Designedly, then, they offered extremely liberal political and religious privileges to prospective immigrants.

It was under the Concessions and Agreement that self-government originated in New Jersey. Each year, on January 1, the freeholders in each town met together and elected two delegates to an assembly. This popularly chosen body, together with the governor and an appointive council of from six to twelve men, made up the general assembly of the province. In this legislature was vested all law-making authority, including the power to constitute courts, provide for defense, enact a criminal code, and prescribe allotments of land. Most important, no taxes could be levied except by the general assembly. The only restraints on the legislature's powers were the provisions that its acts must be consistent with the laws and customs of England and must receive the approval of the Lords Proprietors.

The inhabitants were guaranteed full freedom of conscience in matters of religion, "they behaving themselves quietly and not using this liberty to licentiousness." The general assembly might appoint ministers and provide for their maintenance—which was never done—but the people could in their private capacities support any churches they chose. Such freedom was not common in the colonies, and it had the result of attracting to New Jersey members of a great variety of religious denominations.

The Concessions and Agreement of 1665 also set forth what appeared to be an orderly and generous plan for the distribution of land. As people came into the province, towns were to be laid out for them, with one-seventh of the land in each town reserved for the proprietors and the remainder available to the settlers. Those arriving within the first three years were to have grants of from 60 to 150 acres, with additional amounts for each servant. These were known as "head right" grants. Later arrivals could apply for lands in accordance with such provisions as might be laid down by the proprietors or the general assembly. Each landholder received a patent for his property issued under the seal of the province after the land had been surveyed and the bounds had been officially recorded.

What did the settlers have to pay for these lands? They were not permitted to purchase them outright. Instead, they were required to pay an annual quit rent of a halfpenny or penny an acre, depending on the value of the land. It was this feature of the system that was to cause discontent and disorder. The inhabitants disliked the prospect of never having full title to their homesteads. Moreover, those who had planted the early towns and had purchased their tracts from the Indians with the full approval of Nicolls or Carteret were to maintain that the land system of the Concessions and Agreement did not apply to them. Because the first payments of quit rents were not due until 1670, there were a few years of calm before the storms of dissension arose.

There was little presage of future troubles when the first Assembly convened on May 26, 1668. This historic session, marking the beginnings of representative government in New Jersey,* transacted its business with a minimum of debate in a brief, five-day session at Elizabethtown. The pioneer legislators enacted a severe criminal code, provided for yearly meetings on the first Tuesday in November, and levied a tax of £30—payable in produce—for the support of the government.†

When the second General Assembly met in November, 1668, harmony was replaced by conflict. Delegates from the Monmouth Grant towns refused to take the prescribed oaths of fidelity to the proprietors on the grounds that to do so would jeopardize their rights under their grant from Nicolls. Furthermore, a dispute developed over whether or not the assembly should sit separately from the governor and council. With the delegates stubbornly insisting upon their rights as they understood them, the session broke up in disorder.

This ominous governmental collapse was soon followed by another major crisis. On March 25, 1670, the first payments of quit rents fell due. Down to this time most of the people in the towns had declined to take out proprietary patents for their lands, as prescribed in the Concessions and Agreement. It was their contention that their titles, derived from the grants by Nicolls or from Indian deeds, were quite adequate. Consequently there was an almost general refusal to pay the quit rents. Leading the resistance were the people of Elizabethtown. Two years of prolonged bickering between the governor and his unruly subjects culminated in what amounted to an act of revolution. In May, 1672, an illegally constituted "as-

* In accordance with the privilege conferred in their patent, the Monmouth settlers had an "assembly" of their own which held its first meeting at Portland Point (Atlantic Highlands) on June 4, 1667. Governor Carteret refused to recognize its authority, and it held its last session in 1670.

† The tax was apportioned equally among the six towns. The law did not specify how the tax was to be levied or on what it was to be levied in each town.

sembly" met at Elizabethtown, formally deposed Philip Carteret from the governorship, and elected James Carteret, pliant son of the proprietor, "President of the Country."

With the situation completely out of hand, the repudiated governor sailed back to England to obtain instructions from the Lords Proprietors. This "Revolution of 1672," as it has been styled, was caused primarily by the confusion over land titles arising out of the acts of Colonel Nicolls, but it was undoubtedly influenced as well by the fact that the people of the towns since their arrival in New Jersey had assumed that they were to manage their own affairs. They resented the imposition of any and all restrictions by the proprietors, and they took advantage of every opportunity afforded by the liberal political system and the inherent weaknesses of the proprietors' position to contend for their presumed rights.

Before internal peace could be restored, there came an interruption from an unexpected quarter. Late in 1672 war again broke out between England and Holland, and on July 30, 1673, a Dutch squadron from the West Indies surprised the small garrison at New York and compelled its surrender. For nearly a year New Jersey was once more under the Dutch flag, although the change had little effect on the life of the inhabitants. When peace was restored, the province returned to proprietary control, and Philip Carteret resumed his position as governor in November, 1674.

In the meantime, however, Lord Berkeley had sold his half interest in New Jersey to John Fenwick, who acted on behalf of his fellow Quaker, Edward Byllynge. Subsequently, by the famous Quintipartite Deed of July 1, 1676, the boundary between East and West Jersey was defined as a line running from Little Egg Harbor to the northwest corner of the province. Sir George Carteret retained East Jersey as his exclusive province.

For a few years affairs proceeded quietly in East Jersey. On his return from England, Carteret had brought new instructions that were in the nature of amendments to the Concessions and Agreement. Most significant was the provision that only those who held their lands by a patent from the proprietors were to enjoy the full rights of freeholders. This meant, among other things, that only such men could vote and hold office. Temporarily subdued, the townsmen gave up their former opposition, obediently secured proper patents for their holdings, and began to pay the hated quit rents. Meetings of the General Assembly were resumed, and it seemed that after a decade of instability, the province was at last embarked upon a steady course.

All went well until the year 1680, when once again the province was thrown into political turmoil. This time the difficulties were occasioned by the actions of Sir Edmund Andros, the Duke of York's aggressive governor in New York. For some years Andros had been insisting on the right of his government to tax and regulate the trade of East Jersey, and Carteret had been compelled to acquiesce. Now a more serious issue arose. Andros boldly laid claim to the government of East Jersey in behalf of the Duke.

Philip Carteret sought to resist these pretensions. But on the night of April 30, a party of soldiers sent by Andros seized the hapless governor and forcibly carried him off to New York. There he was ignominiously obliged to stand trial before a court presided over by his nemesis, Andros. Despite Andros' efforts to overawe the jury, Carteret was acquitted of the charge of wrongfully exercising jurisdiction over New Jersey, but he was required to promise not to attempt the resumption of his authority until advice could be obtained from England.

While Carteret awaited a final decision on his fate, Andros added to the confusion by appearing in Elizabethtown to meet the East Jersey Assembly. He read the perplexed delegates his dubious warrants of authority and intimated that they were not to enjoy in the future the full measure of political rights they had claimed in the past. Uncertain of their ground, the delegates were not disposed to clash directly with Andros, but they nevertheless contended stoutly for their rights as freeborn Englishmen. The session concluded abruptly at this point when

Andros had to return to New York. Neither side, apparently, had made any concessions.

The interlude came to an end in March, 1681, when word was received from England that the Duke had repudiated the actions of Governor Andros. Back in power again, Governor Carteret soon discovered that the doubts cast on his authority in the preceding months were not to be readily laid to rest. There had long been an undercurrent of discontent over the changes that had been made in the Concessions and Agreement in 1674. When the General Assembly convened in October, 1681, tempers flared in a heated debate between the aroused delegates and the governor and council. Charging that Sir George Carteret had had no right to amend the fundamental constitution, the representatives went on to challenge the very foundations of the proprietorship. The exchange continued for several days, and in the end Carteret took the unprecedented action of dissolving the legislature. Where this "Revolution of 1681" might ultimately have led remains in doubt, for within the next year East Jersey passed into the hands of a new set of proprietors, and another era in its history began.

In spite of political turmoil, controversy over land titles, and annoyances from New York, East Jersey had become a well established colony. The emigration of people from New York and New England had given it a population of about five thousand, two-thirds of whom dwelled together in the compass of the seven towns. The largest settlement was the capital, Elizabethtown, with perhaps seven hundred residents. Woodbridge was next in size, followed in order by Newark, Middletown, Shrewsbury, Piscataway, and Bergen. Down to this time the fringe of settlement was largely restricted to the lower reaches of the Passaic, the Hackensack, and the Raritan.

The landholding system encouraged a high degree of economic democracy. Most farms ranged between one hundred and two hundred acres in size. A few large grants had been made, mostly to wealthy planters from Barbados, but they were the exceptions to the rule. As yet there was little trade and virtually no industry outside the home. Agriculture was the mainstay of the colonists, and wheat, corn, barley, oats, flax, and garden vegetables were the principal crops. Domestic animals were imported from the neighboring colonies and multiplied rapidly. In the early years there were attempts at raising tobacco in Elizabethtown, and venturesome men occasionally sought their fortunes in whaling, but general farming was to prove the soundest economic activity.

Religion played an important role in the life of the colonists, although the economy of the new country could not support an adequate number of churches and ministers. Most of the people were Puritans, who organized their churches on the Congregational model. Only Newark and Elizabethtown were regularly served by settled ministers; in Woodbridge there were long periods during which no pastor could be obtained. The Dutch Reformed congregation had been organized in Bergen in 1662, but it was not until 1680 that the first church was built there. The Baptists in Middletown and Piscataway did not organize churches before 1688, and it was to be another ten years before the first Anglican clergyman arrived in the province. The Shrewsbury Monthly Meeting of Friends dates from 1670. Because of the extreme shortage of ministers throughout these difficult years, there was doubtless a decline in religious zeal. At the same time, however, there was an absence of the kind of sectarian bickering and intolerance that had marred the history of New England.

Virtually all of the energies of the inhabitants had to be devoted to gaining a livelihood. The planting of a colony required hard toil and left little time for leisure or luxuries, but the settlers had their reward in the sense of accomplishment that came as they saw a wilderness transformed into a region of civilized communities.

The Regime of the Twenty-Four Proprietors

The Carteret period came to an end in 1682, and a new era, bringing with it significant new currents in the development of the province, was begun. The simple pattern of life that had become established was disrupted by the introduction of new elements, which added to the complexities of the social and economic organization of the province. The motive force at the beginning of this period was the desire to make East Jersey a haven for Scottish Quakers. Although the venture was quite unsuccessful, it stimulated the growth of the province in many ways.

The key figure responsible for setting East Jersey on a new course was the great Quaker colonizer, William Penn. Following the death of Sir George Carteret early in 1681, the trustees of his estate put East Jersey up at public auction in 1682. The purchasers were William Penn and eleven English associates, who paid £3400 for the province. Very shortly twelve other men, half of them from Scotland, were brought into the project. Thus East Jersey became the common property of the so-called "Twenty-Four Proprietors," twenty of whom were prominent members of the Society of Friends. On this group devolved Carteret's claims to both soil and government. These rights were recognized and confirmed by the King in March, 1683.

Penn and several of the other English proprietors were deeply interested also in West Jersey and Pennsylvania, and their grand plan was to secure for their coreligionists the whole region between the Hudson and the Chesapeake. Penn at once became so absorbed in his plans for Pennsylvania that he devoted little time to East Jersey, although he did visit the province in 1683. Soon it became understood that the active management of the project would rest with the Scots, and Robert Barclay, the outstanding Scottish Quaker, was made governor of East Jersey. Barclay persuaded many influential Scots, among them the powerful Earls of Perth and Melfort, to purchase shares in the proprietorship and initiated a vigorous advertising campaign to encourage emigration to America.

It was anticipated that vast numbers of victims of the cruel religious and political persecutions then raging in Scotland would grasp the opportunity to emigrate to

East Jersey. Between 1683 and 1685 perhaps five hundred Scots of high and low estate arrived in the colony, most of whom settled in Middlesex, Monmouth, and Somerset counties where in time they came to exercise an influence out of all proportion to their numbers. They were predominantly Presbyterians, and it was largely owing to their efforts that that denomination became established in East Jersey. The ambitious plans made by the promoters of this Scottish colonizing venture were never realized, however, for as persecutions declined after 1685 a major impetus to emigration diminished. Moreover, the promoters lacked the capital required to finance their ventures. Nevertheless, the short-lived project was to add a significant new strain to the already diverse population of the province.

Barclay never came to East Jersey; instead Thomas Rudyard was sent over as deputy-governor late in 1682 to inaugurate the new regime. No important changes were made in the government of the province. The proprietors did concoct a fanciful charter—the "Fundamental Constitution"—but it met with no favor because of its doctrinaire character, and no real attempt was made to impose it on the people. The assembly continued to be a powerful instrument for registering the will of the townsmen, who were ever concerned to defend their "ancient rights" against any unwelcome innovations.

The changes made in the land system were of inestimable importance. Although only one of the original "Twenty-Four" settled in East Jersey, many of them sold fractions of their shares to men who did come over. These "resident proprietors," as they were called, created the Board of Proprietors for the Eastern Division of New Jersey in August, 1684, to administer their vast joint holdings. Membership on the Board was restricted to those owning at least one-quarter of one of the twenty-four full shares. Land was distributed in the form of "dividends," authorized from time to time by the Board. The first such dividend, for example, gave to each holder of a full share the right to take up ten thousand acres of land. Down to 1702 three such dividends, amounting in all to 17,500 acres per full share, were declared. Acreage was allotted in the form of head right grants to new arrivals, and the Board issued many patents for land to non-proprietors, conditional on the payment of annual quit rents.

One of the major consequences of this new system was the emergence of two very different types of landholdings in the province. There were the small homesteads of the early towns, which were held on a quit rent tenure, and there were the vast tracts owned by the individual proprietors. Along the Millstone and the Raritan and in Monmouth County, estates of more than a thousand acres were not uncommon. Many of these huge tracts belonged to absentee proprietors who either leased their holdings or merely kept them for speculation. Thus the basis was laid for a sharp economic cleavage between the yeoman farmers and the landed aristocrats.

This serious divergence was aggravated by a resumption of the old quarrel over the validity of the early town grants. The new proprietors, as had Carteret, chose to regard all titles under these grants as invalid and ignored them in their own surveys. They also renewed the demand for quit rents from those who had been induced to take out patents under Carteret. The result was a constant succession of law suits, riots, and political controversies between the proprietors and their adversaries. Not until after the Revolution did this dispute—still unresolved—die out.

The character of the population also underwent important changes. Down to this time most of the inhabitants had migrated from other colonies. Now there was an influx of English and Scottish settlers, some of them the younger sons of nobility, others humble indentured servants. These new arrivals brought Anglicanism and Presbyterianism to the province. They also added noticeably to the heterogeneity of the population. The center of the new proprietary influence was Perth Amboy, founded in 1683, which became the capital of the province, the home of the proprietary leaders, and the headquarters of the Board of Proprietors.

≈§ 33 §≈

For a few years the new regime went along smoothly. The population increased rapidly, and vast areas in Somerset, Middlesex, and Bergen were brought under cultivation. In the realm of government the old criminal code—harsh in the extreme—was modified under the humane Quaker influence. A new level of government, intermediate between the towns and the provincial authority, emerged with the creation of four counties—Bergen, Essex, Middlesex, and Monmouth—in 1683. In the same year the judicial system made a major advance when the Court of Common Right was created along with county courts similar to the courts that had first appeared in 1675. The vigor of the new administration was also evidenced by the appointment of commissioners to lay out roads, erect jails, and treat with the Indians. There were even negotiations with New York in an effort to determine the precise location of the boundary between the two provinces, but a final settlement of this vexatious question had to wait until 1769. As the population grew and new towns were founded, the size of the assembly was expanded until there were twenty-two delegates in all, representing eleven towns and the sub-county of Somerset.

All seemed well, when suddenly the province was jarred from its course by external difficulties. There was a resurgence of strained relations with New York over the question of customs duties, which New Jersey shippers objected to paying to the collector in New York. More serious was the threat from another quarter. Authorities in England after the accession of James II were meditating a plan for combining all of the northern colonies under a single head. The blow fell on East Jersey early in 1688. Threatened with *quo warranto* proceedings, which would require them to show "by what authority" they pretended to govern, the proprietors yielded up their powers of government to the Crown. The province was then absorbed into the Dominion of New England under Sir Edmund Andros. The practical effect of this move was to leave East Jersey with no functioning government above the local level until the autumn of 1692, when the proprietors regained control.

The final decade of the proprietary period witnessed the virtual disintegration of proprietary authority. Under the governorship of the extremely able Andrew Hamilton, the developing antagonisms between proprietors and townsmen were kept in hand, but when Hamilton was replaced by Jeremiah Basse in 1696, the popular forces erupted. At the core of the matter was the dispute over land titles. In 1695 the proprietors had secured from a friendly court an opinion denying the validity of the Nicolls grants. They then proceeded to harass the hapless townsmen with ejectment suits. Two years later the tables were turned quite unexpectedly when the anti-proprietary faction obtained a decision from the King in Council upholding its claims.

Seizing the initiative, the townsmen extended their land claims at the proprietors' expense and bade defiance to the government. Governor Basse, for obscure reasons, threw in his lot with the popular side. By 1700 there were mass disorders throughout the province, mobs were assaulting the courts, and respect for law was at a low ebb. Even the return of Governor Hamilton did not serve to allay the spirit of rebellion.

These disorders in East Jersey undoubtedly contributed to the decision by the Board of Trade in England late in 1701 to recommend that the province be placed under royal rule. From time to time in the past, particularly in 1680 and 1688, questions had been raised as to the legality of proprietary rule, but no definitive action had been taken. The whole matter is something of a mystery because it should have been perfectly obvious from the outset that the Duke of York could not, under English law, transmit to a third party the governmental powers over New Jersey that had been granted to him by Charles II.

Why the Duke connived in and countenanced the assumption of jurisdiction by the proprietors must remain a subject for speculation and further investigation. Nevertheless, when the Board of Trade came to its decision, the proprietors had no recourse, and on April 15, 1702, they yielded up their pretended powers to Queen Anne, and two days later New Jersey formally became a Royal Colony. The "surrender" involved both East and West Jersey, which were now to be combined as one colony under a royal governor. The proprietors retained their rights to the soil and received other safeguards for their position. But their ill-fated governmental function came to an abrupt end.

The nearly forty years of the proprietary period were marked in many ways by failure. The seeds of dissension between the mass of the settlers and the proprietors had been sown when Nicolls made the grants that were subsequently repudiated by Berkeley and Carteret. Thereafter the problem of confused land titles became a source of disturbance. The fact that the governing authority was in the hands of men who were at the same time concerned with managing vast landed interests was unfortunate, for it meant that political matters were often subordinated and neglected. The main concern of the proprietors was real estate, not government. The frequent changes in control and interruptions in authority certainly constituted a major factor of instability. Moreover, the proprietors, lacking the prestige that attached to royal government, were quite unable to keep in check the strong popular forces that found expression through the democratically based assembly. When the tides of English policy turned against the principle of proprietary governments, the tottering regime was doomed.

The failures of these years, however, should not be permitted to obscure the positive developments. It was in this era that the firm foundations of representative self-government were laid in New Jersey. Later generations acknowledged their debt to the Concessions and Agreement of 1665, which came to be regarded as the original source of rights and privileges. It was during this period, too, that lasting institutions of town and county government began their course of development, that the boundaries of the present state were described, that the cleavage between East and West Jersey—still evident today—was ordained.

Economic patterns of enduring character were also fixed. All land titles in East Jersey today—with the exception of those in the contested areas of the Nicolls grants—derive from proprietary patents. Indeed, such unclaimed land as remains today can be obtained only through the agency of the Board of Proprietors, which still maintains its office in Perth Amboy. The dual character of the land system—the small holdings of the townsmen in contrast to the large estates of the proprietors —long exerted an influence on the economy and society of the colony and the state.

The heterogeneous nature of the population of New Jersey in the twentieth century had its counterpart in proprietary days. The liberal conditions of settlement promulgated by Berkeley and Carteret attracted people from many lands, who brought with them a variety of religious beliefs. Tolerance and understanding soon reinforced legal guarantees of freedom. East Jersey was not, strictly speaking, an "English" colony; it was planted by people from Holland, Belgium, Finland, France, Germany, Ireland, Scotland, Sweden, and Wales, together with New Englanders and those from England. From the first years of settlement, Negro slaves in increasing numbers labored under the supervision of their white masters. No colony offers better materials for the study of the process of "Americanization" than New Jersey.

III

WEST JERSEY:
QUAKER COMMONWEALTH

WEST JERSEY REPRESENTED THE PRODUCT of the vision
and enterprise of the Society of Friends, or, as they are
more commonly called, the Quakers. It was, in fact, the
first Quaker colony in America, antedating Pennsylvania
by several years. It was a very different colony from East
Jersey, not only in the sources of its population and its
underlying religious character, but also in its economic
and social organization. It was, on the whole, less subject to violent internal dissension than its neighbor, but
it also suffered from frequent changes in governmental
authority. Perhaps its most significant and lasting characteristic was the pervasive influence of the liberal and
humane Quaker philosophy.

FOUNDING THE QUAKER HAVEN

The Quakers trace their origins to the early preaching
of their greatest spiritual leader, George Fox, around the
middle of the seventeenth century in England. Not until
1668 did the sect actually develop a settled form of
church organization. Believing in the vital importance of
an inward religious experience and opposing all ritual-
ism, ostentation, or "worldliness," the Quakers immediately found themselves at odds with every other denomination in England. Their refusal to pay tithes,
swear oaths, or bear arms similarly brought down upon
their meek heads the wrath of the civil authorities. For a
quarter of a century—until the passage of the Toleration

Act in 1689—they were made the victims of relentless persecution. Quaker missionaries who ventured into Puritan New England as early as 1656 met a hostile reception; four of them were hanged in Boston by 1661. In England as late as 1685 there were 1300 Quakers in prison. One does not have to look far to discover what motivated these people to seek a haven of refuge in the New World.

Some Quakers had settled in Shrewsbury in 1664, and others followed them in subsequent years to the tolerant province of East Jersey. George Fox is known to have visited these small bands of Friends on his journey to America in 1672. Doubtless these circumstances had some bearing on the interest shortly manifested by the harassed English Quakers in planting a colony in New Jersey. A rare opportunity was presented to them in 1674 when Lord Berkeley abruptly decided to sell his half-interest in the province, which up to that point had yielded him no profit.

The nominal purchaser of Berkeley's rights—for the bargain price of £1000—was Major John Fenwick, a member of the gentry who had been a soldier under Cromwell and who had recently become a Friend. Fenwick was actually an agent for Edward Byllynge, also a Quaker, who was a close friend of Lord Berkeley. Byllynge was a man of large affairs in London, engaged in the brewing business, but he was at the time in serious financial straits and could not negotiate the purchase in his own name. So involved were his finances that three prominent Quakers—William Penn, Gawen Lawrie, and Nicholas Lucas—took over the management of his property in the capacity of trustees until his many debts were discharged.

Byllynge and his associates devoted nearly three years to planning how their colony might best be developed as a refuge for their coreligionists. One difficulty that confronted them was the failure of the Duke of York to confirm their purchase. Until this should be done, their authority to exercise powers of government over their domain lay under a cloud. Moreover, no division line had yet been established between their holdings and those of

Carteret. This matter was handled by the Quintipartite Deed of July 1, 1676, between Sir George Carteret and Penn, Lawrie, Lucas, and Byllynge. It was agreed that the boundary line should run from Little Egg Harbor to the northwest corner of New Jersey. The colonial architects were also engaged in drawing up a model constitution—the Concessions and Agreements—and in bringing the attention of Quakers throughout the British Isles to their ambitious venture.

It was decided to divide the ownership of the province into one hundred shares, or "proprieties," and sell these shares to prospective Quaker colonists. Within a few years, over one hundred men became shareholders, some of whom owned only a fraction of a share. The usual purchase price was £350 for a share. In subsequent years, as the shares were subdivided into quarters, sixteenths, thirty-seconds, and even smaller fractions, the number of proprietors increased greatly. It was the understanding of the purchasers that they were acquiring not only the right to participate proportionately in the distribution of the land of West Jersey, but also that as joint proprietors they were collectively to possess the governmental authority that had formerly been vested in Berkeley. For his services in connection with the acquisition of Berkeley's interest, John Fenwick was allotted ten of the original one hundred shares.

The careful planning of the leaders of the project was rudely upset when Fenwick impatiently decided to settle the holdings to which he was entitled without waiting for the main body. Accordingly, he proceeded to offer land for sale and organize an expedition; and in November, 1675, he arrived with his party on the ship *Griffen* in the Delaware. There he established the town of Salem—the first English community on the Delaware—and sought to set up his own queer form of government. Immediately he ran afoul of Governor Andros in New York, who properly insisted that, inasmuch as the Duke of York had not yet confirmed Berkeley's sale, the Quakers had no right to exercise governmental powers. To add to his difficulties, Fenwick had left his affairs in England in a tangled condition. The result was that after several involved transactions, Fenwick found himself possessed of only the land within his immediate little colony, his remaining interest in the ten shares having passed into the hands of William Penn. Within a few years Salem, or Fenwick's Colony, had been absorbed in the general Quaker commonwealth.

Finally, all the necessary preliminaries having been arranged, the main colonizing effort was ready to get under way. A group of several substantial Quakers from Yorkshire, who had acquired ten proprieties, together with a group of shareholders from London, set sail from England in the *Kent.* As they moved down the Thames, they passed King Charles II, who was diverting himself aboard his barge. Coming alongside the *Kent,* the King inquired whether all of the passengers were Quakers and gave the company his royal blessing. After a tedious voyage, the passengers—230 in number—together with their household equipment and their stock, landed near Raccoon Creek in August, 1677. There they remained for some weeks, relying on the hospitality of the few Swedish families in the vicinity, while final arrangements were being made for their removal to the lands that had been selected as their permanent abode.

Before their arrival in the Delaware, the expedition had taken the precaution of stopping at New York to confer with Governor Andros. There the several "Commissioners" who had been appointed in England to manage the enterprise, pending the establishment of regular government under the Concessions, encountered their first major obstacle. Andros pointed out that technically the settlers remained under his jurisdiction until the hoped-for confirmation by the Duke arrived. But he agreed to commission as local administrators of the area the same men who had been designated by the body of proprietors. Some of these commissioners then proceeded overland to the Delaware, in advance of those on shipboard, to select sites for settlement. With the aid of Swedish interpreters they successfully negotiated with the Indians for the purchase of the lands along the river from

Oldman's Creek to the falls of the Delaware (Trenton). After further consultation, the London and Yorkshire people agreed to engage jointly in founding a town; and the place that they selected became Burlington.

The Yorkshiremen chose as their "tenth" the lands between the new town and the falls; the London "tenth" was laid out from Burlington southward. The dividing line between the two tenths was High Street, Burlington. When the town was surveyed, each owner of a full share received a home lot of ten acres and a farm of about sixty-four acres adjoining the settlement. Because of the lateness of the season, the colonists were unable to make adequate provision for the winter, and most of them were forced to live in wigwams, constructed after the Indian manner, and depend for their sustenance on Indian corn and venison purchased from the friendly natives. When spring arrived, they began the construction of permanent houses and the development of their farms.

Within the succeeding few years, nearly fifteen hundred immigrants—most of them Quakers—arrived in the province. One group, from Dublin, Ireland, in 1681 laid out the "Irish tenth," which later became Gloucester County. The flow of new settlers slackened decidedly after 1682, for by that time the colonization of Pennsylvania was under way, and it soon became the focal point of Quaker interest under the vigorous direction of William Penn. Among the earliest arrivals were men mainly of middle-class background, with a preponderance of tradesmen and craftsmen over agriculturalists. The purchase of even a quarter of a propriety represented a very considerable investment, and the cost of transporting a family and goods across the ocean was no small amount. The price of passage for an adult was figured at £5. Those who came as "servants" would customarily work for their masters for four years, at the end of which time they would receive ten bushels of corn., wearing apparel, two hoes, and an axe. They would then be free to make their own way in the New World.

The high aspirations of the Quakers for their commonwealth were well expressed by the planners of the project: ". . . there we lay a foundation for after ages that they may not be brought in bondage, but by their own consent, for we put the power in the people . . ." These democratic ideals permeated "The Concessions and Agreements of the Proprietors, Freeholders and Inhabitants of the Province of West New Jersey in America." Drafted in March, 1677, the Concessions even today are striking for their liberal and humane provisions and deserve to be studied by all who are interested in the roots of American liberty.

This remarkable document placed almost unlimited political power in an assembly elected by all the proprietors, freeholders, and inhabitants. Elections were to be held annually according to a unique system of secret balloting. When the province had all been divided into tenths, there would be ten delegates from each subdivision, or a total of one hundred in the assembly. The assembly would choose ten "Commissioners of State," who were to manage provincial affairs when the legislature was not in session and to oversee the distribution of land. There was no provision for an upper house, for a governor, or for a veto power by the proprietors; the only limitations on the legislature were that all acts must be consonant with English law and must not conflict with the Concessions.

The personal rights of the people were shielded by elaborate safeguards against tyranny or injustice. Asserting that "no man, nor number of men on earth, hath power or authority to rule over men's consciences in religious matters," the Concessions set forth the strongest possible guarantees of religious freedom. No person was to be deprived of life, liberty, or estate without a due trial before a jury of twelve good men of his neighborhood. There could be no prosecutions without formal indictment, no proof of crime without the testimony of two honest and reputable witnesses. Any accused person could serve as his own lawyer. Trials were to be held in public, in order that justice would not be "done in a corner nor in any covert manner." To the end that all inhabitants might know their rights, copies of the Concessions were to be posted in every courthouse and read in public four times a year. Here, indeed, the power was to be in the people.

To the great disappointment of the scores of proprietors who had purchased shares in the province, this model constitution was never to be put wholly into effect. When the Duke of York, in 1680, finally confirmed the sale to the Quakers, he conferred the powers of government exclusively on Edward Byllynge, who named himself governor of the province. Byllynge never came to America; instead he sent over a deputy-governor. The proprietors, who had assumed from the beginning that they had purchased the government as well as the soil of West Jersey in common, felt that they had been cheated, but they were compelled to accept the situation. Now the Concessions did not, of course, make any provision for a governor. Moreover, Byllynge was not legally bound to recognize them. But in general, and most particularly with respect to the guarantees of civil and religious liberties, the framework and spirit of the Concessions were followed. The popularly chosen assembly retained large powers, although it was curbed somewhat by the presence of a governor and a council.

The land system designed by the Concessions was subjected to even more drastic alterations. Originally it was intended that the province would be surveyed into ten equal parts or "tenths," and that each tenth would be further sub-divided into ten "proprieties." As proprietors moved into the province, they were to take up their proportionate holdings, settling each tenth in order. Provisions were also made—as in East Jersey—for head right grants, subject to the payment of a quit rent, but such holdings were rare. It was in accordance with this arrangement that the Yorkshire and London tenths were peopled. But the system broke down almost immediately; some tenths were never surveyed, and soon proprietors were permitted to select their lands wherever they chose.

For several years the distribution of land was under the supervision of ten commissioners, who were elected by the assembly after that body came into existence. Then in 1688 the proprietors agreed to establish a council, chosen by themselves, to discharge this function. This body, the Council of Proprietors of the. Western Division of New Jersey, was made up of nine members, five chosen at Burlington and four at Gloucester. Any proprietor who owned so much as one thirty-second of a share was entitled to vote and hold office. As was the case in East Jersey, the Council periodically declared dividends. The first one gave each holder of a full share the right to take up 5200 acres. Others followed from time to time; the last one—the seventh—was declared in 1859. When a dividend was declared, each proprietor would become entitled to warrants, or rights, for the acreage due him. He could then request the surveyor-general or his deputy to survey either all or a portion of the amount specified in the warrant. When the Council had approved this survey, it was recorded in the proprietary records and the transaction was completed. No deed or patent was issued. Many proprietors sold their warrants for around £10 a hundred acres instead of actually taking up the lands in their own right. The Council has continued in existence down to the present time, with its office and ancient records still in Burlington, and continues to authorize surveys of previously unclaimed land.

Under this system, it was relatively easy for anyone in West Jersey to acquire land; there was less of a tendency for a small number of large shareholders to monopolize land than was apparent in East Jersey. The average landholding in West Jersey was perhaps two or three times the size of that in East Jersey; farms of three hundred acres and more were common. Too, because of regulations in the early years requiring that surveyed lands must be occupied within three years, absentee ownership was discouraged. On the whole, the system functioned in a fairly democratic manner and did not unduly limit economic opportunity.

During its career of less than three decades as a proprietary colony, West Jersey had the misfortune to experience five major shifts in the source of governmental authority. Under such circumstances it is remarkable that the province exhibited as much political stability as it did. Only the strength of local institutions at times prevented a complete descent into anarchy. The story of this period, then, is a confusing one, but beneath the confusion may be discerned solid accomplishments in the day-to-day life of the people.

As the first settlers went about their tasks of building their homes and seeking their livelihood, they reluctantly acknowledged their temporary subordination to Governor Andros in New York and awaited the day when the Duke of York would permit them to have their own government. Meanwhile, they annually elected ten commissioners, most of whom received Andros' approbation, to conduct public business. When at last the news arrived that the Duke had acted, but that he had conferred the government on Byllynge alone, there was great consternation and resentment.

Byllynge had commissioned as his deputy-governor Samuel Jennings of Buckinghamshire. Jennings, a man of unusual attainments, was zealous in his defense of democratic principles and often during his career of nearly thirty years at the forefront of West Jersey political affairs was a center of controversy. He was generally admired among the Quakers, and did not hesitate to challenge any person in authority when he felt moved to do so. He arrived in the province with his family late in 1680, and in the following year met with the first Assembly. With Jennings' approval, the legislature as its first business adopted what amounted to a new constitution, which accorded the governor little power and restated the major provisions of the discarded Concessions. The governor could not veto laws, make any appointments, dissolve the Assembly, make war, or levy taxes.

When Jennings agreed to accept these conditions, the assemblymen consented to acknowledge him.

For two years all went well. An impressive body of legislation dealing with such important concerns as the regulation of land distribution, the levying of taxes, the establishment of the courts in Burlington and Salem on a regular basis, the authorization of fairs and markets, and the laying out of highways and designation of ports occupied the attention of the Assembly. The lawmakers even dealt with such matters as fixing the sizes of bricks to be made in the province. Of especial interest was one law decreeing that a quantity of Irish half-pence brought to West Jersey by Mark Newbie, one of the settlers of the Irish tenth, should serve as local currency. Newbie became, in effect, the first banker in the province.

Meanwhile, however, resentment was growing against Byllynge, and in 1683 at a general meeting of the freeholders—which was attended by William Penn—a quiet revolution took place. The meeting resolved to demand that Byllynge relinquish his powers of government to the general body of proprietors and proceeded to elect Jennings governor of the province. The following year Jennings and Thomas Budd were instructed to go to England to carry the dispute with Byllynge to a conclusion. When these emissaries reached London, they were induced to submit the issue to the arbitration of several "weighty Friends." After hearing both sides, the arbitrators concluded that Byllynge's legal claims could not be set aside but that he should endeavor to rule in accordance with the Concessions. With great reluctance the settlers yielded to this award and accepted Byllynge's new appointee, John Skene, as their deputy-governor in 1685.

Scarcely had this crisis passed when another arose. Byllynge died and his heirs sold his considerable interest in the province—together with the government—to Dr. Daniel Coxe in 1687. Coxe, an Anglican, was a court physician who engaged on a tremendous scale in colonial speculations. The Quaker proprietors and inhabitants were understandably concerned about the prospect of coming under the rule of a non-Quaker, but Coxe indicated that he would make no drastic changes in the government of the province. With a great burst of energy, he promoted the establishment of a whaling company at Cape May and a pottery at Burlington and planned numerous other grandiose activities. But his ambitious schemes were never realized.

Before Coxe could make his authority effective, West Jersey was in 1688 absorbed into the Dominion of New England under Andros. For the next few years the government of the province was virtually suspended. To further complicate matters, just as the dominion era came to an end, Coxe decided to abandon his West Jersey project. In 1691, he sold most of the 22 shares that he had accumulated—and his governing powers—to the West Jersey Society, in which body the governing powers remained vested until the end of the proprietary regime.

The West Jersey Society, which now became the owner of about twenty proprietary shares in the province, was made up of 48 men, most of whom resided in or near London. Their purchase was made solely as a business venture. They anticipated that by selling lands and engaging in trading ventures, they could reap a handsome profit from their investment. Their holdings included interests in East Jersey and Pennsylvania as well as in West Jersey. Members of the company had no thought of emigrating to America; rather, an agent was retained to manage the company's real estate in the provinces. Controlling the largest single block of shares by far in West Jersey—the only other considerable holders of multiple shares were the Penn and Coxe families—the Society soon acquired enormous tracts of land. Its Minisink Patent included two hundred thousand acres; there was another tract of ninety-five thousand acres in Hunterdon, and a third that included most of Cape May County. The Society was active until 1814, when it disposed of its remaining interests to Benjamin B. Cooper, and it retained its corporate identity in England until it was finally liquidated in 1923. Obviously, it was to play a large role—both economically and politically—in the history of West Jersey.

The officers of the Society were not inclined to engage actively in ruling West Jersey. They appointed an extremely able governor, Andrew Hamilton—who held the same position in East Jersey—and permitted the people to conduct their public affairs much as they had in the past. Perhaps the most significant feature of this new regime is that it brought to an end the completely Quaker domination of West Jersey and resulted in the introduction of non-Quakers—principally Anglicans—into positions of prominence. Over the years since 1681, many non-Quakers had settled in West Jersey, and the strength of this element was augmented after 1692 when, as a result of a serious religious controversy, large numbers of Quakers broke away from their sectarian affiliation. What had once been a thoroughly homogeneous community now became sorely divided into two increasingly distinct groups.

Under the astute Hamilton, potential friction between these two parties was held to a minimum. But in 1698 Hamilton was succeeded by Jeremiah Basse, a resourceful adventurer who immediately aroused the bitter hostility of the Quaker element by his shady dealings and his unconcealed antipathy toward them. Led by their respected champion, Samuel Jennings, the Quakers refused on various pretexts to recognize Basse's authority. Factional strife mounted and the province became divided into two hostile parties. Even the return of Hamilton in 1699 did not quiet the discord, for now the adherents of Basse took the offensive and claimed, with some basis in fact, that Hamilton's powers rested on dubious grounds.

As the century drew to a close, then, the proprietary governments in both East and West Jersey had degenerated through internal discord to a condition verging on anarchy. Frequent shifts in authority had so confused and weakened the position of the proprietary governor that he was no longer able to command respect or maintain order. The hopeful experiment in self-government that had been envisioned in the Concessions had eventuated in spiteful quarreling, riots, and chronic instability. It was at this point, appropriately enough, that the officialdom in England saw fit to inquire into the fundamental question of the legal right of the proprietors to exercise powers of government.

The proprietors in both Jerseys were not unaware of the fact that their claims to exercise powers of government rested on no sound legal foundation. Moreover, they were now leaning to the view that their property rights might be better safeguarded under the rule of a royal governor than under their own ineffectual regimes. Consequently they were disposed to surrender their political pretensions in return for guarantees that would secure their economic interests. The Board of Trade, which was the effective instrument for determining colonial policy in England, heard the views of the proprietors on this question, but understandably took the position that the surrender of authority must be unconditional. Therefore in April, 1702, the two sets of proprietors jointly "surrendered" their powers to Queen Anne, and the Queen "graciously accepted."

The Jerseys had ceased to be proprietary colonies and were now united as a royal colony, under the jurisdiction of the Crown. Although the surrender was in theory unconditional, in fact the Queen was to embody in her instructions to the first royal governor most of the conditions that had been requested by the proprietors. Strict adherence to these terms would not only secure the property rights of the proprietors but give them effective political control as well. At the moment it seemed that the proprietors had turned their apparent defeat into a major victory.

THE QUAKER COMMUNITY

The turbulence that marked the political affairs of West Jersey was in contrast to the solidity and serenity that characterized the daily life of the Quaker inhabitants. Religion was a strong force in West Jersey, and the peculiar tenets and form of organization of the Society of Friends molded a distinctive community. Even after the Society declined in relative numbers and in spiritual vigor, the counties along the Delaware retained a cultural flavor that set them apart from the Puritan counties to the north.

The Quakers were better able to transport their religious institutions to the New World than most denominations were, because they were not hampered by the requirement of a trained ministry or by any dependence on a remote hierarchy. As soon as they landed in Salem and Burlington, they established meetings for worship, initially in private homes and shortly thereafter in plainly-designed meeting houses. As the area of settlement expanded, new meetings were readily formed. In time, an effective system for holding the several meetings together in a common framework was instituted. Monthly Meetings were organized to handle the "outward" or business affairs of the membership, supervise the local meetings for worship, and guard the conduct and morals of the people. Several Monthly Meetings would send delegates to a Quarterly Meeting which would settle problems arising from the Monthly Meetings. Over all was the Yearly Meeting. Beginning about 1684 the several "Quarterlies" on both sides of the Delaware sent delegates to this annual session, which served as the general governing body of the denomination. Until 1764, Yearly Meeting was held alternately in Burlington and Philadelphia; thereafter it was fixed in the larger city. With this simple but all-embracing scheme of organization, it was possible for the Quakers to serve all their members and maintain discipline and uniformity.

Quakerism deeply affected the daily, temporal living of its adherents. Plainness in dress and speech, sobriety, frugality, modesty, and industry were strongly enjoined on all members. When any Friend strayed from the discipline, he would be visited by a delegation from the Meeting, and if this caution did not suffice, he might risk the shame of being expelled from the congregation. Marrying "out of meeting" was strongly discountenanced.

Children reared in accordance with the traditional precepts were given a "guarded" education and were taught to shun frivolity and worldly diversions. More than any other denomination in the colonies, the Quakers were readily distinguishable not only by their doctrine, but also by their speech, dress, and mode of living.

The Quaker community was not, despite its peaceful tendencies, free from religious discord. In 1692 it was greatly disturbed by a controversy that resulted from the preaching of George Keith. Keith, who had come to East Jersey in 1685 as surveyor-general, soon became one of the most influential Quaker leaders in the colonies. His increasing tendency toward orthodox Christian theological positions brought about his repudiation by the main body of Friends. Many, however, remained loyal to Keith and followed him in his independent course. When some years later Keith joined the Anglican Church and returned to New Jersey as a missionary of that Church, he once again attracted many converts. Both the Keithian schism and the growth of Anglicanism destroyed the religious unity of West Jersey. Moreover, the immigration that occurred after 1685 was substantially non-Quaker. Perhaps by 1702 no more than half of the inhabitants of the province were Quakers. But Quaker mores continued for another century to influence the cultural pattern of the Delaware valley.

Excluded from many forms of leisurely diversions by their religious tenets, and shunning idleness and vice, the Quakers devoted their energies to their farms and shops. It is not surprising that within two generations they accumulated substantial properties and became noted as successful businessmen. Although a high proportion of them had come from non-agricultural pursuits in England, they quickly adapted themselves to the opportunities afforded by the abundant and cheap land of the new country.

THE WEST JERSEY FRONTIER

It is interesting to observe that in West Jersey the general movement of the frontier was from west to east;

from the broad highway of the Delaware into the interior along the course of the numerous streams that emptied into the river. By 1702, there was a well-settled strip nearly twenty miles wide extending southward from Trenton to Delaware Bay. Here was good soil, gently rolling and well watered, and crops were easily transportable by small boats to nearby markets. On the Atlantic coast, there were small settlements at Cape May, made up chiefly of Baptists from New England who were engaged in fishing and whaling, and a sparse Quaker population in the vicinity of Egg Harbor. The interior section of the colony, the region of the sandy pine barrens, was not attractive to settlers and offered little of economic value except timber.

The main occupation of the people was, of course, farming. Wheat, corn, oats, rye, flax, and hemp were favorite crops, with rice and cranberries something of a specialty in Salem. Livestock, imported from England and the older colonies, multiplied rapidly. On the larger farms, indentured white servants and Negro slaves toiled in the fields or performed the menial household tasks. Horses and hogs were permitted to run in the woods, and the latter soon became so numerous as to constitute a nuisance and a menace. Many men found profitable occupations in the fur trade, in fishing and whaling, in the production of pitch, tar, and resin, and in cattle raising. Tradesmen of all kinds followed their crafts, especially in the few larger towns. To facilitate the exchange of commodities within the province, weekly markets were established by law at Burlington and Salem as early as 1682. Overseas commerce, which began when Mahlon Stacy sent his ship to Barbados in 1680, was encouraged when Burlington and Salem were designated as ports for entering and clearing vessels. Despite such occasional calamities as the crop failures in 1682 and 1687 and the disastrous flood at Trenton in 1697, the inhabitants made amazing progress in building a sound and varied economy.

The province must have presented an attractive picture of prosperity in a rural setting at the end of the century. The crude dwelling places of the first settlers had been replaced by sturdy brick houses, narrow-fronted but deep structures that seemed unnecessarily cramped in the broad countryside. Split-rail fences zig-zagged across the landscape, marking off fields and pastures. At many crossroads stood the plain, rectangular, brick Quaker meeting houses.

The chief town, Burlington, was a scene of bustling activity. Vessels laden with beef, pork, and breadstuffs sailed from its commodious wharf bound for Philadelphia and the West Indies. To its periodic fairs and markets came farmers and tradesmen from the surrounding countryside. Its streets were lined with stately brick houses, and on the outskirts of town was the notable "palace" of John Tatham, surrounded by delightful gardens and orchards. At the center of activity was the imposing market house, on the second floor of which was the hall where the legislature met. Nearby was the prison. Malt-houses, brew-houses, bakeries, craftsmen's shops, and taverns added to the urban character of the provincial capital. The sole religious structure was the meeting house, an unusual hexagonal building topped by a cupola and having a long wing extending from one of the sides. Not until 1703 was St. Mary's Church, the first Anglican church in the province, built in the town. The Quaker experiment in creating a new society in the wilderness had succeeded, even though political strife, religious dissension, and a sharp decline in Quaker immigration prevented the fullest realization of the original plans for the colony.

THE PROPRIETARY HERITAGE

During the nearly four decades that New Jersey was under proprietary regimes, fundamental political, economic, and social patterns emerged that were to have a lasting influence on the subsequent history of the province. This was the period when our basic institutions were developing, and it is to these years that we must look for the roots of our heritage.

It cannot be too strongly emphasized that almost from the moment of their arrival, the colonists enjoyed unusual opportunities for learning the difficult lessons involved in self-government. They brought with them from England a respect for law, a strong belief in individual liberties, and considerable acquaintance with the forms of representative government. In both East and West Jersey they looked to written constitutions with their basic guarantees as the safeguards of their freedoms. They came to insist that their fundamental laws could not be cast aside; they perceived that their best security lay in a government of laws and not of men. They soon constructed a framework of government, which in its broad outlines has persisted to the present time. Resisting all attempts at the imposition of arbitrary authority, they never gave up their struggle to make the voice of the people heard through their duly elected representatives. On another level, they worked out satisfactory ways of conducting public business in the county and township. Looking beyond the factional controversies and the periodic breakdowns and shifts in proprietary authority, one must be deeply impressed with the lasting contributions of the proprietary period to our political development.

In an agrarian economy, the method of land distribution is an important factor. Very early in both Jerseys diverse landholding systems appeared. There were the relatively small acreages of the townsmen of East Jersey, the somewhat larger farms of the West Jersey yeomen, the large estates of the proprietors, and the enormous tracts held by the Penns, the Coxes, and the West Jersey Society. Because land was the chief form of wealth, economic classes, often with conflicting interests, reflected the unequal size of landholdings. But it should be recognized that in spite of the proprietors' monopoly of land, it was not difficult for any man to acquire a homestead of his own. Attempts to create semi-feudal estates, worked by renters or servants, were conspicuously unsuccessful. Whether by strictly legal means or otherwise the ambitious man could make a plot of ground his own. Thus individual enterprise, rather than feudal manorialism, was to be the mainspring of economic activity.

The social complexion of the Jerseys was characterized by an extraordinary variety of nationalities and religions. In marked contrast to New England or the southern colonies, New Jersey opened its doors wide for all to enter, and offered the liberal political and religious provisions to attract all peoples. The remarkable fact is that in an age not distinguished for tolerance or for international sympathies, this heterogeneous population experienced no dangerous social tensions. Even though the Dutch in Bergen clung to their native speech for considerably more than a century, and the Quakers in Burlington persisted in their refusal to serve in the militia, and the Puritans of Newark held to their stern moral code, such diversity did not produce serious dissension. These settlers, each group with their own peculiar ways and beliefs, somehow learned lessons of tolerance and goodwill that their ancestors across the Atlantic had not mastered. One might say simply that they were all learning to be Americans.

It would be misleading to depict the Jerseys as one general community. In fact, there were sharp contrasts between East and West Jersey, contrasts which have not disappeared even today. The sources of settlement of the two provinces were quite distinct; each had its own government, its own proprietary land system. The fact that each had a separate existence for some three decades was not going to be erased instantly when the provinces were united in 1702. The population of East Jersey was much more varied than that of West Jersey. In the former province the people were compactly settled in townships, whereas in West Jersey the farms were widely dispersed. East Jersey was much more seriously divided by internal quarrels, arising out of the peculiar complexities of the dispute between the early townsmen, with their quit rent obligations, and the proprietors. There was no comparable source of contention in West Jersey. No small factor in emphasizing the cleavage be-

tween the two divisions was the growth of the cities of
New York and Philadelphia, which rapidly drew within
their respective orbits the adjacent sections of New Jersey. Certainly an important and continuing heritage
from the proprietary period is the distinction that we
presently observe between what we now call North Jersey
and South Jersey.

IV

THE ROYAL PROVINCE, 1703-1763

WHEN THE PROPRIETORS MADE THEIR "SURRENDER" to
the Crown in 1702, a distinctly new era began in the political history of New Jersey. The two Jerseys were reunited to form a single royal province. The source of all
governmental authority passed from the inept hands of
the proprietors to the ponderous bureaucracy in England that assisted the monarch in exercising his prerogative powers. Political experimentation of an extreme sort
was succeeded by a type of constitutional stability that
in time came to be regarded as excessively restrictive.
For many decades, despite frequent friction between the
peoples' representatives and officials of the Crown, the
new political order met with general acceptance. Only
when Parliament sought to introduce innovations that
threatened long-prized liberties did the colonists become
restive. Ultimately they concluded that they were compelled to choose between their ancient loyalty to the
mother country and their own conception of their fundamental rights, between subservience and independence.

THE PROVINCIAL GOVERNMENT

As New Jersey assumed the status of a royal province,
the structure of its government underwent drastic
changes. In common with similar appendages of the
Crown elsewhere, it was brought within the orbit of the
several agencies of the English government that participated in colonial administration; many of its officials
were made royal appointees, and its constitution, in ef-

fect, was determined by the commissions and instructions of the royal governors. Self-government was not abolished, but it was greatly curtailed.

The English system of colonial administration was bewilderingly complex and unwieldy, with the result that inefficiency, indecision, and procrastination prevailed. Under the Crown, the Privy Council nominally made important decisions of policy. Actually the Board of Trade, a hard-working agency staffed by men having a practical knowledge of colonial problems, furnished guidance to the Privy Council. The Board of Trade in turn received information and counsel from several agencies and individuals. Complicating the picture was the fact that many bureaus other than the Board of Trade had important responsibilities for colonial administration. The commissioners of customs, the lords of the treasury, the lords of the admiralty, the lords of justice, the bishop of London, and the secretary of state for the Southern department all affected the government of the colonies. Because administration was not centralized, responsibility was divided and urgent problems might go unsolved for years while various officials jealously guarded their authority.

The representative of the Crown in the colony, and the central figure in colonial administration, was the royal governor. In theory, at least, the King might have empowered his representative to govern in a completely arbitrary manner, without an assembly or other vestige of popular participation. But in all the royal colonies it became customary to grant a measure of self-government in accordance with provisions set forth in the commission and the instructions that each governor received when he assumed office. These documents may be loosely regarded as the constitution for the province, although the instructions contained many directions for the governor that were not constitutional in nature.

In New Jersey, the structure of the provincial government was directly influenced by the negotiations that took place between the proprietors and the Crown representatives prior to the "surrender." The proprietors had requested that the two Jerseys be combined into a single government and that the legislature should meet alternately at the two old capitals, Perth Amboy and Burlington. They further proposed that each division should have equal representation on the governor's council and in the assembly, that Perth Amboy and Burlington should each be accorded two representatives, that the franchise should be restricted to those owning one hundred acres of land, and that an estate of one thousand acres should be required of those who sat in the assembly. They also urged that full civil and religious liberty be granted to all Protestants. In order to safeguard their land interests, they asked that they be permitted to name the surveyors-general in their respective divisions, that they have the exclusive privilege of purchasing lands from the Indians, and that their land claims and rights to quit rents be confirmed. All of these terms were subsequently embodied in the commission and instructions of the first governor, except the last one, and in this case the governor was directed to have the legislature enact a law to accomplish the desired objective. The request of the proprietors that they be permitted to nominate the first governor was not granted. It will become evident that the proposals made by the proprietors—especially those relating to the system of representation and the high qualifications demanded for voting and holding office—were calculated to give them a preferred political position in the province.

The functions of the several branches of the provincial government remained fairly stable down to the time of independence. The royal governor had many important roles to fill. He was the chief executive, the commander-in-chief of military forces, chancellor, and ordinary. He could convene, prorogue and dissolve the assembly and order new elections whenever he chose. He appointed most provincial officials, such as judges, justices of the peace, sheriffs, and coroners, and had a voice in naming members of his council. He had a veto power that could not be overridden by the legislature. Despite his broad authority, however, his position was not a strong one.

His powers were largely defensive; that is, he could block measures, but he could not secure positive action without the assent and cooperation of the assembly. Above all, because the legislature alone enjoyed the right to levy taxes, the representatives of the people, not the governor, controlled the purse strings. All too frequently, governors found themselves in the awkward position of having to try to serve two very different masters. They had to obey their instructions from the Crown, but they had also to yield to the pressures exerted on them by the assembly. Moreover, because of the administrative confusion in England, the governor often had to wait years before he knew what action was to be taken on particular matters or before he could get urgently needed advice.

The governor's council was usually made up of twelve members appointed by the Crown, with equal numbers from East Jersey and West Jersey. The councilmen were drawn largely from the ranks of the principal proprietors and they exerted a conservative influence in provincial affairs. They served as an advisory group to the governor, who was obliged to seek their counsel on all major questions. In addition, the council was the upper house of the legislature and sat in a judicial capacity as the highest court of appeal in the province. On most issues the council sided with the governor, but, like the chief executive, it was obliged to recognize the need for harmonious relations with the lower house.

The assembly was the popular organ of government, and by jealously defending and expanding its privileges it was able to more than hold its own in any contest with the governor. Initially there were ten members chosen at large from each division and two each from Burlington and Perth Amboy, but after 1705 each of the seven counties was allotted two representatives, as were the twin capitals and the town of Salem. There was no fixed time for holding elections. If the governor chose, he might keep the same assembly for several years. On the other hand, he might order more than one election within a single year if he thought that by doing so he might obtain a body more subservient to his wishes.

The assembly's greatest source of strength lay in the fact that it could give or withhold money for projects that the governor or the authorities in England advocated. Not only could it block any legislation, it also had the power to initiate laws and then bargain with the council and the governor to secure their approval. It could even deprive the governor and other officials of their salaries, although this threat was rarely carried out. Once a law had been enacted and sent to England, it might be approved, disallowed, or held in abeyance. Certain important classes of laws, such as those relating to trade and currency, were often passed with suspending clauses, which meant that they were not to take effect until they had been specifically approved by the Crown.

The judicial system was defined by an ordinance promulgated by Governor Cornbury and his council in 1704. At the local level, justices of the peace and the county courts had limited jurisdiction in civil and criminal matters. Above these courts was the supreme court, with both original and appellate jurisdiction. The highest court in the province consisted of the governor and council, which heard appeals from the supreme court. Presiding over all cases involving equity was the governor, acting as chancellor. In his capacity as ordinary, the governor possessed a type of ecclesiastical jurisdiction over matters relating to the probating of wills and the administration of estates. In exceptional cases, appeals could be taken to England. The legislature had no part in constituting or regulating the courts, for this was an area within which the Crown chose to exercise its prerogative.

Relatively few important changes were made in the nature of the government throughout the royal period. Perhaps the most significant development had to do with the governorship. Down until 1738, New Jersey shared its governor with New York. As might have been anticipated, the royal appointees tended to devote the greater part of their time to the affairs of New York, with the result that public affairs in New Jersey suffered from neglect. Finally, after years of persistent agitation, New Jersey was given its own governor.

With the creation of new counties as the population expanded, the composition of the assembly was altered. By 1775 there were thirteen counties, each with two as- semblymen, and in addition two members each were chosen from Perth Amboy and Burlington. The powers of the assembly were subtly extended from time to time in minor ways, but frequent efforts to secure the regular election of assemblies on a triennial or even a septennial basis met with unyielding opposition.

Viewing the new political structure broadly in comparison with that which had existed during the proprietary period, certain obvious differences can be noted. Popular self-government ostensibly suffered a setback, and at the same time democratic influences were curbed. No longer could the unruly and aggressive representatives of the small freeholders dominate and even overturn the government. But the apparent loss of political freedom was perhaps counterbalanced by the stability of the new regime. Furthermore, as has been pointed out, the assembly remained a powerful organ of the popular will. The worst features of royal rule probably resulted from the faulty coordination between the provincial authorities and those in England, which often led to inept administration and unrealistic policy-making. The great virtue of royal rule, as matters developed, was that it permitted the people to acquire the experience with techniques of self-government that they were to apply so ably to their public affairs after 1775.

FACTIONS AND POLITICS

The political scene during the royal era was seldom dull and often tempestuous. The legislature frequently was divided into rival factions which resorted to every sort of tactic to gain their respective ends. Even more commonly, the governor and the assembly were at odds over a host of matters ranging from fiscal policy to personalities. In such clashes, both sides had their choice of several available weapons, with the result that combatants were evenly matched and the battles often indecisive in their outcome. Much, of course, depended on the personality of the royal governor. If he was tactful, shrewd, and skilled in the art of politics, he could often command the respect and cooperation of the assembly without unduly compromising his own authority. But if he was stubborn, arrogant, inept, or indifferent, he would soon be made to feel the strength of his adversaries. Although the theme can be overemphasized, it is nevertheless true that much of the political controversy of this period can be viewed as a tug-of-war between the governor and the assembly, with each side seeking either to defend or extend its powers.

It was unfortunate that the new regime was inaugurated by a governor who lacked almost every qualification for coping with the political tensions that carried over from the proprietary period. Edward, Lord Cornbury, was the black-sheep son of an illustrious family. A cousin of Queen Anne, he had dissipated his fortune in England and had procured the governorship of New York and New Jersey for the purpose of attempting a speedy rehabilitation of his finances. His extraordinary personal habits made him an object of ridicule, and his extravagance and corruption were notorious. As a climax to his career in the colonies, he was placed in a debtor's prison as soon as he was removed from the governorship.

When Cornbury met his first assembly at Perth Amboy in November, 1703, he was immediately made aware of the fact that the province was divided into several discordant factions. Arrayed together on one side were the influential resident—or "Scotch"—proprietors of East Jersey, the Quaker group from West Jersey, and the spokesmen of the West Jersey Society. In the opposite camp were the anti-quit rent townsmen from Essex and Monmouth, the "Anglican" faction from West Jersey —headed by Colonel Daniel Coxe, Thomas Revell, and Jeremiah Basse—and the "English proprietors" of East Jersey under the wily leadership of Peter Sonmans. This latter clique, which represented many non-resident proprietors, favored the rapid disposal of proprietary lands for immediate gains, whereas the "Scotch" proprietors preferred to manage their common holdings so as to produce the greatest profit over a long period. Essentially, the contest was to be between two rival proprietary parties, with the townsmen of East Jersey aligned for reasons of expediency against their old enemies, the Scottish proprietors.

In the first election the Scotch faction used brazenly unfair tactics to assure victory for their side. By managing to hold the election in a remote area, they were able to make their small forces effective against their more numerous adversaries. In control of the assembly, they then sought to push through a set of laws favorable to their interests, including one that would have confirmed their title to the soil and also their right to collect quit rents. But when they refused to vote the governor an adequate income, he withheld his approval from their acts.

Cornbury now resolved to throw all his influence on the side of the Sonmans-Coxe party. Doubtless this decision was motivated by the fact that a large bribe, known as the "Blind Tax," had been presented to him to gain his favor. Dissolving the antagonistic assembly, he ordered another election to afford his new associates an opportunity to win control. When this second assembly met and it became evident that Cornbury's friends had again been defeated, the governor refused to seat three Quaker members on the flimsy pretext that they lacked the necessary qualifications. The purged house then proceeded to ride roughshod over the Scottish-Quaker party, lowering voting qualifications, enacting a militia law that bore heavily on the Quakers, and levying taxes that fell chiefly on the large landowners. When the three Quakers were finally seated at a later session, a deadlock ensued between the governor and the assembly, which he sought to break by holding a new election.

The third assembly, which convened in 1707, contained a large majority hostile to Cornbury. When the governor asked, as usual, for adequate financial support, the lower house responded by launching a thorough investigation of the governor's public and private conduct. Leading the attack were the Speaker of the House, Samuel Jennings, the redoubtable Quaker who had first gained prominence as the opponent of Edward Byllynge's governmental pretensions, and Lewis Morris. Morris, who was to be the outstanding political figure in New Jersey until his death in 1746, possessed large estates in both New York and New Jersey, was a prominent member of the East Jersey Board of Proprietors, and acted as agent for the West Jersey Society. In the course of his political career of more than half a century, he sat both in the assembly and on the council, served as a justice of the supreme court, and in 1738 became Governor of the province. An aristocrat and a firm servant of the Crown, he was under Cornbury to play a popular role in opposition to corruption and tyranny.

In an address to the Queen, Morris, Jennings, and their associates recited the many evil actions of the wretched governor, including his acceptance of the "Blind Tax" and his refusal to permit the three Quaker members to be seated in the second Assembly. In addition they described how Cornbury and his confederates had sought to enrich themselves through shady land deals. By devious means, the Cornbury "Ring," as it was called, had secured control of the offices of Surveyor-general and Registrar in East Jersey and also succeeded in gaining exclusive possession of the proprietary records. They then proceeded to award themselves immense tracts of land. In West Jersey, Daniel Coxe and his Anglican adherents used equally questionable tactics to dominate the Council of Proprietors there. The entire picture was a sordid one, both in the political and the economic realms. Stirred at last by these protests, the English authorities removed Cornbury from office in 1708. During his tenure only nine laws had been enacted, and six of these had subsequently been disallowed. The government had been kept in turmoil, the proprietary land system had been thrown into confusion, and lasting enmities had been aroused between the rival factions.

The task of bringing order out of this chaos fell to Governor Robert Hunter, who took office in 1710 after the brief regimes of John, Lord Lovelace, and Richard Ingoldsby. Hunter was an able man with a military background, influential connections, and a moderate fortune. As soon as he understood the situation in New Jersey, he determined to side with the Scotch-Quaker party. The old Cornbury Ring, now led by Daniel Coxe and Peter Sonmans, with the connivance of Jeremiah Basse, was still influential in the council. Hunter sought and received from England permission to replace these men with his own favorites, including Lewis Morris. For a time all went well. With a harmonious council and assembly, Hunter succeeded in having enacted a host of belated laws, among them one which removed any question about the ability of Quakers to hold civil offices.

Then an unexpected development upset this smooth combination. Queen Anne died and was succeeded by George I in 1714. Tradition decreed that on the death of the sovereign, a new election should be held for members of the assembly. Coxe and his associates seized this opportunity to carry on an intensive campaign in West Jersey, and when the seventh Assembly convened in 1716, Coxe was in control. Hunter tried the familiar tactic of dissolving the assembly and ordering another election, but Coxe again won, and Hunter had the unpleasant task of recognizing his adversary as the speaker of the house. Coxe and his faction then embarked on a program of obstructionism, calculated to embarrass the governor. But when they went so far as to refuse to attend a session of the legislature, Hunter rounded up sufficient members to organize the assembly and then had the absentee members declared in contempt and expelled. When new elections were held to fill the vacated seats, Hunter's party won undisputed control of the house. The power of the Coxe faction was broken forever. Coxe went to England in an effort to obtain Hunter's removal, but his mission was a failure. When he left the province, he was succeeded as president of the West Jersey Council of

Proprietors by Lewis Morris. The new order was then secure.

With the downfall of Coxe and his allies, the province entered upon a period of relative tranquillity in the political arena. Hunter sailed home to England in 1719 with the boast that he left New Jersey in peace, a striking contrast to the maelstrom he had found when he first arrived. The Scottish and Quaker proprietors held positions of leadership in both houses of the legislature as well as in their respective proprietary organizations. In East Jersey, where the proprietary Board was strangely lethargic, bold schemers like Dr. John Johnstone, George Willocks, and others engaged in intricate land deals at the expense of their associates. The West Jersey Council sought to undo some of the actions of the Coxe regime and permitted Lewis Morris, agent for the West Jersey Society, to assume a dominant role in prosecuting the interests of his distant clients. The morality of both boards, it might be observed, was strongly akin to that of the later age of the "robber barons," and there is considerable evidence that proprietary affairs and politics were closely intertwined.

Robert Hunter's successor as governor, William Burnet, was the eldest son of the famous Bishop Gilbert Burnet and a godson of William and Mary. A literary dilettante with an open, sociable manner, he was disposed to follow the course of least resistance in discharging his governmental responsibilities. After some early clashes with the real political leaders of the province, he saw the necessity of coming to terms with the assembly. A fortunate marriage soon after his arrival relieved him of his financial anxieties, and the adoption of the loan-office plan in 1723 similarly solved the financial problems of the province. Thereafter, the governor collected his salary regularly and permitted the assembly more latitude than it had ever before enjoyed. Under the able leadership of John Kinsey, Jr., an aggressive liberal who lost no opportunity to extend the boundaries of self-government, the assembly even induced the governor to approve laws—later disallowed—reducing official fees and providing for elections every three years. It is little wonder that when Burnet moved on to the governorship of Massachusetts in 1728, his departure was widely lamented in New Jersey.

Under Governors James Montgomerie (1728-1731) and William Cosby (1732-1736), the assembly continued to hold the center of the stage. Cosby, whose tactless behavior involved him in serious difficulties in New York, met the New Jersey legislature only once. Receiving an appropriation to cover his salary for the ensuing five years, he saw no necessity of calling another session.

Cosby's troubles in New York, however, were to have repercussions in New Jersey. In brief, he became involved in a bitter fight with Lewis Morris, who in addition to his many offices in New Jersey was also Chief Justice of the Supreme Court of New York. The result of this controversy was that Morris sailed for England in 1735 determined to have Cosby removed and secure a separate governor for New Jersey. After more than a year of lobbying, he was forced to conclude that his mission had been a failure. But Cosby's death in 1736 compelled the home authorities to reconsider the question of the governorship. After the usual delays, a decision was reached. New Jersey should have its own governor and Lewis Morris should be the first royal appointee.

When Morris assumed office in 1738, it was generally expected that with his demonstrated ability, his unequaled experience, and his strong principles he would be an ideal governor. But he was now an old man, cantankerous and unyielding, and few governors had worse relations with the legislature. Because Morris was fully aware of all the tricks employed by assemblies in the past to frustrate royal governors, having originated many of the maneuvers himself, he dealt more sternly with the lower house than any of his predecessors. At the same time he rigidly upheld every one of the powers that he believed belonged of right to his office.

A determined struggle resulted. The assembly cut Morris' pay, insisted on controlling not only the appropriation but also the disbursement of funds, declined to levy taxes, and refused to enact desired laws unless the governor would pledge his support to popular measures that the Assembly had proposed. Morris in turn used his veto power frequently, threatened to refuse to sign warrants for the assemblymen's pay, resisted all attempts to bribe him, and, on occasion, berated the assembly in the strong language that he employed with scalding effectiveness. Toward the end of his administration, the revival of the ancient land controversy between the East Jersey proprietors and the townsmen led to riots and tumult and greatly complicated the problems confronting the aged governor. When Morris died in 1746 after thirty-five years of public life, there were few to lament the passing of a man who today stands forth as the most remarkable figure in the history of the province.

The disturbances arising out of the land riots constituted the major issue facing Morris' successor, Jonathan Belcher. A native of Massachusetts, Belcher came from a prominent mercantile family, entered political life after his graduation from Harvard, and served for a dozen years as governor of Massachusetts. He was a politician, ever inclined to moderate differences and bend to the winds of opinion. When he discovered that most of the political factions in New Jersey—with the conspicuous exception of the powerful East Jersey proprietary clique —sympathized with the small landowners in their conflict with the landed aristocracy, he prudently sided with the majority.

The assembly did little or nothing to put down the disturbances, and Belcher accepted their inaction and himself did no more than appeal to England for instructions. In these circumstances the council, which stood forth as the sole champion of the proprietary interest, sought to prod the governor, without effect. There resulted the unusual spectacle of the governor and assembly siding together against the council. In the long run, Belcher's strategy was probably sound, for the riots gradually subsided after 1755. Had the government undertaken the repressive measures that some proposed, there might well have been a "revolution" reminiscent of that of 1672.

By 1757, when Governor Belcher died, attention had been diverted from the local land disturbances by the far larger problems arising out of the French and Indian War. This great conflict, which rapidly assumed world-wide proportions, had its origins in the long struggle for supremacy in North America between France and England. The fourth in a series of wars between these two aggressive nations, this one, like its predecessors, placed the colonies in peril and imposed on them heavy military obligations. Throughout most of the decade that ended with the Peace of Paris in 1763, New Jersey was called on to furnish men, money, and supplies for the military effort. Because the province was not itself directly in danger of invasion, the people did not appreciate the urgency of the cause, and the legislature was ever reluctant to do all that was requested of it by the royal authorities.

In this time of crisis, three governors held office in too-rapid succession within a period of six years. Governor Francis Bernard (1758-1760) was an unusually able executive, but he was soon transferred to Massachusetts. Governors Thomas Boone (1760-1761) and Josiah Hardy (1761-1763) were weak appointees, and the latter was recalled from his office because of a flagrant violation of his instructions with regard to the manner of appointing justices. Each governor had as his main duty the formidable task of inducing the legislature to assume the province's fair share of the burden of imperial defense. Never disposed to place a heavy tax load on its constituents, the assembly was usually both tardy and niggardly in complying with the governor's wishes. Moreover, the legislators would agree to additional expenditures only on the condition that they be financed by the issuance of paper money. Despite the pleas and remonstrances of the royal authorities, this policy was followed consistently.

In extenuation of the legislature's position, it should be noted that New Jersey's troops suffered a succession of disastrous experiences in the war. Half of the provincial regiment was captured at Oswego. Later, after its ranks had been filled, most of its men were made prisoners at Lake George. Then, in the heavy fighting at Ticonderoga, the regiment once more incurred numerous casualties. Such incidents did not heighten the province's enthusiasm for the war effort.

In addition to maintaining a regiment, the province was also called upon to furnish money for the general campaigns, to build five barracks—one of which still stands in Trenton—for housing fifteen hundred men, and to construct blockhouses for the defense of its own northern frontier. Fortunately, incipient Indian raids into the northwestern corner of the province were brought to an end by the Treaty of Easton, negotiated in 1758, by the terms of which compensation was given to the Indians for their remaining land claims. Although the legislature made the most of its bargaining position throughout the conflict, it nevertheless contributed a large amount, in proportion to its resources, to the war. Because it refused to levy taxes, it piled up a staggering debt of nearly three hundred and fifty thousand pounds in bills of credit. By 1765, New Jersey had the largest debt of any of the colonies.

FACING THE ISSUES

While the governor and the assembly were carrying on their habitual contest for supremacy, the provincial government was compelled to deal with real problems. Even in that relatively simple age, some two centuries ago, government had important and necessary functions to perform. Many of these were of a routine nature, such as laying out highways, regulating tavern fees, providing justice, creating new counties and townships, or incorporating religious and charitable institutions. Other matters involved large questions of public policy and directly affected the welfare and the economic interests of all the inhabitants. A brief examination of certain of these major issues will reveal some of the most pressing political concerns of the period.

The most difficult problems with which the legislature

had to deal—then as now—lay in the field of finance. Money had to be raised to meet the ordinary expenses of government and—all too frequently—to aid in the several Anglo-French wars. Resort to heavy taxation was never popular. Moreover, the problem was complicated by the fact that there was little "hard money"—gold or silver—in the province at any time. Because New Jersey, like the other colonies, tended to buy more goods from England than she sold, an unfavorable balance of trade and a consequent shortage of specie resulted. Thus two considerations were intertwined. How could revenues be provided for governmental needs and how could an adequate supply of money be kept in the province?

The most highly favored solution to this problem was the loan-office system. In essence, the provincial government established a land bank, printed paper currency, lent this currency to borrowers who gave mortgages on land for security, collected interest on these loans, and then used the interest to meet governmental expenses. The plan was first tried in New Jersey in 1723. The sum of £40,000 in paper money was loaned in amounts averaging £35 for a period of twelve years. Each county was assigned a quota that its inhabitants might borrow. Interest was fixed at 5 per cent, and the loans were to be amortized over the twelve-year period. The loan-office bills were made legal tender; that is, they had to be accepted at face value for all debts. Under this arrangement, the province was assured of a steady income from the interest payments, borrowers secured money at low interest rates, and a sound money supply was created. Significantly, all classes within the province heartily endorsed the loan-office system from the royal governor down to the humblest yeoman.

The success of this first experiment led to the establishment of a second loan office in 1733. This time the amount was £20,000; the loans were to run for 16 years, and the interest was specifically dedicated to the support of the government. A third loan office in 1735 for £40,000 followed similar principles. Thereafter, down to the eve of the French and Indian War, there were no provincial taxes in New Jersey. The interest money financed all the costs of government.

One difficulty with the system was that as the principal on a loan was paid off, this money would customarily be retired from circulation. Consequently, as the years passed, the supply of money shrank, a distressing deflation resulted, and demands arose for another loan office. After 1740, however, British policy was opposed to further issuances, because British merchants objected to accepting the bills as legal tender. For nearly thirty years the assembly repeatedly passed loan-office measures only to have them disallowed in England, despite the endorsement that these acts usually carried from the royal governors. In time, this issue became one of the major grievances of the province against the home government. Finally, in 1774, a fourth loan office in the amount of £100,000 was approved, but only with the unsatisfactory provision that the bills should be legal tender for taxes alone.

Another device that was employed to finance the government was the issuance of bills of credit. Paper money, with no backing either in land or specie, was issued, usually with the proviso that it be retired by taxation within a brief span of years. The fact that the bills were receivable at face value for taxes made them generally acceptable. This expedient was first tried as early as 1709, but the issues were for small quantities down to the French and Indian War. Then the assembly, reluctant to impose sufficient taxes and prevented from creating a new loan office, indulged heavily in the issuance of bills of credit. Altogether the wartime flood of paper reached a peak of £342,500, most of which was authorized with the provision that the bills be retired by taxes within five years. Obviously the tax burden in the postwar years was formidable, and as the money was withdrawn from circulation, the whole economy felt the effects. All local authorities agreed that the loan office offered the best solution to the province's financial problems.

Another important subject that required legislative attention was the system of elections. Cornbury's initial instructions set high property qualifications both for voting and for holding office and specified that ten representatives should be chosen at large from each division of the province and two from each of the capital towns. The proprietors frankly regarded these conditions as essential to the maintenance of their own political supremacy. Almost immediately there were demands for more liberal qualifications, to which Cornbury gave encouragement. In 1709, a new election law significantly broadened the franchise and made the several counties the basis of representation. All freeholders possessed of real estate *or* personal property worth £50, current money, were permitted to vote. Similarly, assemblymen must have estates of £500 in real or personal property. A year later, assemblymen were required to be residents of the county from which they were elected. Not until 1725, curiously enough, was there any legislation specifying how elections were to be conducted. Existing custom was largely ratified by a law which provided that the sheriff should be in charge of the poll in each county, that the poll should be moved from place to place until all had had an opportunity to vote, and that voice voting—rather than ballots—should be employed. Recognizing the existing electoral abuses, the law forbade bribery or intimidation of voters. The election system functioned with a minimum of difficulty, and in practice gave to each landowner a voice in the representative process.

Of quite a different character was the problem the provincial lawmakers faced in attempting to define New Jersey's boundary with New York. In the original grant to Berkeley and Carteret in 1664 it had been clearly stated that one end of this boundary should be at 41° latitude on the Hudson River. The other end of the line was to be at the northernmost branch of the Delaware River "which is in forty-one degrees and forty minutes of latitude." Now the difficulty was that there was no branch of the river in that precise latitude, and the question was whether to adhere to the latitude description or to accept some branch of the river in the vicinity. The problem was further complicated by the fact that one terminus of the boundary between East and West Jersey was to be this ambiguous northwest station point. During the proprietary period there had been unsuccessful efforts to secure agreement on this point, but the unacceptable Keith Line, run in 1687 from Little Egg Harbor to the south branch of the Raritan near Three Bridges, was the only tangible result.

The matter rested for many years until, in 1719, the legislatures of New Jersey and New York appointed commissioners to locate the boundary. An agreement was signed recognizing a point on the Fishkill in latitude 41° 40′ as the northwest station point, but disagreements developed on other issues, and no line was run. With the movement of population into the northwestern portion of the colony, the East Jersey proprietors became increasingly insistent that the disputed boundary be clarified in order that a correct dividing line could be run between their lands and those of West Jersey. When no action was forthcoming, they took the initiative and in 1743 had their surveyor, John Lawrence, mark a boundary line from Little Egg Harbor to the point on the Fishkill that the commissioners had fixed in 1719. West Jersey, however, refused to give official recognition to this *ex parte* act. Several more years of delay followed. Meanwhile, there were frequent affrays in the border area between inhabitants variously claiming to be under the jurisdiction of New York or New Jersey.

At last, after the two provinces had agreed to submit the dispute to arbitration by the Crown, a royal commission was appointed in 1767. Two years later the case was heard and a decision was rendered. The northwest station point was set several miles south and east of the place determined in 1719 at 41° 21′ 37″ at the junction of the Delaware and the Neversink. Although both New York and New Jersey were dissatisfied with this award, they accepted it, and the boundary line was finally run in 1772. By this determination, New Jersey lost over one hundred and fifty thousand acres to which she had formerly laid claim.

Once the new northwest station point had been fixed,

the West Jersey proprietors sought to have the legislature recognize it as the correct terminus of the boundary between East and West Jersey. Such a new line would have added nearly half a million acres to West Jersey at the expense of East Jersey. The so-called true line was never drawn, but Lawrence's line gained tacit acceptance by both sets of proprietors.

The ancient controversy between the East Jersey proprietors and those who sought to possess land on the basis of the old Elizabethtown titles or direct purchase from the Indians continued to produce discord within the province. It was the policy of the proprietors to hold their common lands off the market in order to keep the value of their private estates high. Meanwhile, as the population of the province grew, increasing numbers of settlers were determined to have their own homesteads, regardless of the restrictive practices of the proprietors. A crisis developed after 1734 when the Elizabethtown Associates, having won a favorable court decision over the proprietors, took the offensive. In flagrant disregard of the proprietors' rights, the Associates conveyed titles to lands in Somerset County near Basking Ridge.

After trying numerous ejectment suits against the intruders, the proprietors determined to seek a definitive settlement of the issue in a momentous test case to be instituted in the Court of Chancery. Three years were spent in preparing the necessary bill, setting forth the lengthy history of the dispute. The bill was filed in 1745, and the Elizabethtown Associates then undertook to prepare an answer, which was not completed until 1751. While these ponderous legal maneuvers were under way, tensions between the opposing camps grew to the point where violence broke out.

In 1745 one Samuel Baldwin of Newark was jailed on a charge that he had cut wood on lands claimed by the proprietors. This event stirred the local citizens to rally to Baldwin's defense, and they assembled together in defiance of the local authorities and released the prisoner from his confinement. Within the next few years, there were similar incidents in Middlesex, Somerset, Morris, and Hunterdon. The rioters soon developed a powerful organization throughout the northern counties and even extending into West Jersey as well. Jails were wrecked, sheriffs and judicial officers were threatened, armed bands took vengeance on those who held titles from the proprietors, and law enforcement agencies were quite powerless to deal with the emergency.

When Governor Belcher arrived in the province, he found the assembly unwilling to take any drastic steps to halt the riots, and he prudently took the expedient course of asking for advice from the authorities in England. The council, which was under proprietary control, fumed at the governor's complacency, but could do little more than register complaints against him. No practical instructions were forthcoming from England, and the riots proceeded. In 1752 there was another turbulent jail delivery in Perth Amboy, and in Hunterdon the tenantry was boldly defying the landlords.

With the outbreak of the French and Indian War, the riots subsided and new problems engaged popular attention. But the disorders had clearly indicated the weakness of the provincial government in failing to maintain law and order. The governor had no troops at his disposal, no constabulary, no effective power over the militia. Doubtless these lessons were remembered by patriot-leaders two decades later. As for the long-awaited suit in the Court of Chancery, it never came to trial. The proprietors apparently were content to let well enough alone when the riots subsided. In any event, the basic issues—dating back to 1665—have never been judicially determined.

Some brief reflections on these six decades of royal rule are pertinent here. It should be clear that New Jersey—like her sister colonies—accepted her subordination to British authority with no very strong manifestations of discontent. Because the assembly was a potent instrument of representative government, little could be done in the colony that did not have a fair measure of public acceptance. The royal governors and the administrative agencies in England might negate actions of which they disapproved, but their powers of initiative were negligible. Not until Parliament began to enact legislation which directly affected the internal concerns of the colonies and impaired their traditional autonomy after 1763 did colonial restiveness become acute.

Royal rule, it should be noted, brought with it many salutary consequences. It enabled the people to continue to acquire experience in the techniques of self-government, experience that was to prove invaluable when the decision for independence was made. Membership in the British empire also conferred inestimable advantages on the young settlements in matters of trade, defense, and intercolonial affairs. Too, royal rule assured a degree of political stability that had been notoriously lacking during the proprietary regime. In brief, these years may be viewed as an essential period of incubation, under highly favorable conditions, preceding the birth of a new state in a new nation.

V

THE COLONIAL SCENE

WHILE THE PEOPLE of colonial New Jersey were wrestling with their complex political problems, they were at the same time equally involved in the many tasks incidental to providing themselves with a satisfactory manner of living. For all classes of society there were economic, religious, cultural, and social concerns no less absorbing than those relating to government. Here were individuals and families seeking to achieve their personal needs and aspirations. Here, too, was a new and expanding population almost unconsciously engrossed in the process of constructing a functioning society. Colonial life was dynamic and colorful. Each succeeding decade broadened the panorama of daily existence.

PEOPLE AND PLACES

The most striking characteristic of the population of New Jersey in the eighteenth century was its extraordinary diversity. An unsophisticated traveler passing through the province might have been startled to discover many areas where Dutch, German, Swedish, or French was more commonly spoken than English. He would also have noticed the strong traces of Scottish, Welsh, or Irish dialects in other regions. The presence of Negro slaves, many of them speaking the language of their Dutch or German masters, would have only increased his doubts as to whether he was indeed in an "English" colony. As a matter of fact, if he had made a thorough survey of the white population on the eve of the Revolution, he would have found that slightly less than half were English in their origins. Somewhat over one-sixth of the people traced their roots back to Scotland, Ireland, or Wales, another sixth was Dutch, about one-tenth was German, and there were smaller proportions of Swedish, French, and other national stocks. Perhaps one-twelfth of the total population was made up of Negroes, all but a small number of whom were slaves.

The population of the province had multiplied many times since the inauguration of royal rule. In the absence of reliable census reports, any figures for this period are merely approximations, but they indicate a steady rate of growth. The population was estimated at fifteen thousand in 1702. By mid-century this number had quadrupled, to sixty thousand, and by 1775 it had risen to one hundred twenty thousand. Roughly, the population doubled each generation. In the third quarter of the century the rate of increase was slowed somewhat because more people were leaving New Jersey for new homes in the west or in other colonies than were entering.

The distribution of the population between East Jersey and West Jersey was nearly equal, but the seven northern counties contained over three-fifths of the people. The most populous county was Hunterdon, closely followed by Burlington, Monmouth, Essex, Morris, and Sussex. Cape May with fewer than two thousand inhabitants brought up the rear.

Bergen and Somerset were the strongholds of the Dutch. Migrating from New York early in the eighteenth century to the fertile valleys of the Hackensack, the Passaic, and the Raritan, the Dutch brought with them a tradition of industry and thrift, a strong desire to cling to their native tongue and their reformed Church, a marked lack of interest in politics, and a propensity toward slaveholding. Well into the middle of the nineteenth century, the Dutch language, greatly corrupted, continued to be used in the home and in the church. Predominantly farmers, with little inclination toward other economic activities, they accumulated large landholdings to divide among their numerous sons.

The Scotch-Irish were especially prominent in the hills of Somerset and Morris, although many were to be found also in the newer lands of Hunterdon and Sussex. Morris County had a strong New England flavor, and down to the time of the Revolution continued to receive a steady stream of new arrivals from Massachusetts and Connecticut. According to one observer, the Yankees, when compared with the Dutch, "affect more gentility, are more apt to run in Debt, to scheme and speculate, more litigious, and have more Genius and Learning, fond of Arms, Liberty and Democracy."

The Germans, who were relatively late arrivals, settled chiefly in Hunterdon and Sussex. Many came as indentured servants, and others secured their economic start as tenants on the large estates in those two counties. With agricultural practices far in advance of their British neighbors, they won an excellent reputation as farmers, and soon acquired homesteads of their own. Middlesex and Monmouth contained small but distinguishable groups of Scots, who furnished many men to the learned professions and to politics. The southern counties were overwhelmingly English in background, although Cape May was another outpost of New England as was also a segment of Cumberland. In Salem and Gloucester were many descendants of the early Swedish colonists, still distinctive enough to support their own Swedish Lutheran Church.

The variety of the origins of the population would afford an excellent opportunity for surveying the distinctive cultural contributions of each group, but the subject has been too little explored. We are, however, readily made aware of the differences in domestic architecture, many of which may be attributed to the origins of the settlers. In Bergen there were the characteristic Dutch colonial houses, showing strong Flemish influences, with hipped roofs, projecting eaves, and sturdy brownstone walls. Typical of the Raritan valley were the long, story-and-a-half, peaked-roofed frame houses of the Dutch farmers of that region. Many of the early dwellings in Morris were built on the familiar plan of the Cape Cod cottage, and similar influences were visible in Cape May. The Quaker counties of Burlington and Gloucester, with their high, narrow, brick dwellings, offered still another architectural style, and Salem was distinctive for its intricate brickwork designs and the dates and initials ornamenting the ends of houses.

The fact that the English settlers customarily made no effort to stable their cattle or use manure for fertilizer, while the Germans followed both practices; that the Scotch-Irish settled in the hills and the Dutch in the valleys; that the New Englanders were avid politicians and the Germans were not—these and many other significant contrasts are evident among the different national and cultural stocks and would repay further investigation.

The distribution of the population within the province was strongly influenced by geographical factors, of which the most important was the location of navigable streams. In an age when land transportation was difficult and expensive, water routes were highly important. Moreover, there were usually associated with the streams well-watered farmlands and pastures as well as the water power essential for sawmills, gristmills, and similar enterprises. New Jersey was unusually favored in having a great many sizable creeks and rivers draining into both the Delaware and the Atlantic. From an early date the valleys of the Hackensack, the Passaic, and the Raritan were populous and prosperous farm regions, with ready water access to the markets in New York. Similarly, the Rancocas, Big Timber, and Oldman's creeks, and the Cohansey and Maurice rivers—all flowing into the lower Delaware—made possible convenient travel to Philadelphia. The Mullica River and the Great Egg Harbor River afforded the inhabitants of the vast "pine barrens" their best highways for transporting their wood and iron products. The only important town in New Jersey that was not situated directly on a navigable stream was Elizabethtown, and it had its port facilities a few miles distant on Newark Bay.

Although all but a small fraction of the population lived under extremely rural conditions, New Jersey by

1750 boasted five incorporated cities—Elizabeth, Perth Amboy, New Brunswick, Trenton, and Burlington. In addition, Newark was a town of considerable importance, and Princeton, Bordentown, Salem, Bridgeton, Freehold, Bergen, Hackensack, and Morristown were hamlets containing from fifty to one hundred houses.

Elizabeth, with perhaps twelve hundred residents in 1775, was the largest municipality in the province and one of the most attractive. Its houses, most of which were shingled, were well spaced and surrounded with orchards and gardens. Its two spelndid churches—Anglican and Presbyterian—were considered by a foreign visitor in mid-century to be superior in appearance to any in Philadelphia. A handsome town hall, topped by a spire; the immense stone barracks; and the graceful mansions of the Daytons, the Ogdens, William Livingston, and Elias Boudinot gave the city an air of dignity and maturity.

Newark, which enjoyed the honor of being the county seat of Essex, rivaled Elizabeth in size. Surrounded by apple orchards, the town straggled for nearly two miles along Broad Street. It, too, boasted two churches and had an excellent academy, a spacious "training ground," and a picturesque setting between the winding Passaic River and the Orange Mountains. Despite its early pretensions to commercial greatness, Perth Amboy had not realized the ambitions of its founders and had scarcely seven hundred inhabitants. Stronghold of Anglicanism, residence of many influential proprietors and government officials, one of the twin capitals of the province, and a port of some consequence, Perth Amboy was a seat of culture and gentility and a bastion of conservatism.

Its neighbor and rival, New Brunswick, was a relatively "new" town, having been chartered in 1731. Profiting by its location at the head of sloop navigation on the Raritan, it was the market town for the prosperous valley and had many prominent merchants and storekeepers among its thousand residents. With two churches, a courthouse, a barracks, a market house, a grammar school, and a college, it left a favorable impression on the stream of visitors who passed through on the main highway that led from New York to Philadelphia.

Princeton, with scarcely sixty houses, would have been without distinction except for the imposing presence of Nassau Hall and some exceptionally fine residences, among them that of Richard Stockton. It was also the halfway point for many of the stages that traversed the province. Not far distant, on the banks of the Delaware, was Trenton, with about one hundred families. Located at the falls of the river, it did a thriving business in transshipping the cargoes of wheat that were floated down the river in the large, shallow-draft Durham boats. Several ferries and noted taverns gave evidence of its importance as a transportation center.

Some twelve miles down the river was Burlington, once the most prominent town on the river but now living quietly under the shadow of Philadelphia. Prosperous Quaker merchants mingled easily with communicants of venerable St. Mary's Church, and elegant houses—some the summer residences of wealthy Philadelphians—graced the river bank. Only when the legislature was in session or the West Jersey proprietors met could the town recapture the prestige it had enjoyed several decades before.

Each of the towns that has been described owed some measure of its importance to its location on the main highways that ran across the province between the key cities of New York and Philadelphia. Although water transportation was virtually the only practicable means of carrying commodities, travelers often preferred to go by land because of the vicissitudes of tides and winds. By the end of the seventeenth century, Lawrie's Road had been opened from South Amboy to Burlington, and John Inian had marked out a thoroughfare that ran from Trenton to Elizabeth and Newark, by way of Princeton and New Brunswick. After 1765, when a road was constructed across the meadows from Newark to Paulus Hook, this newest route had more traffic than any other. The Old York Road, which led eastward from Lambertville to New York, and the King's Highway, from Burlington to Salem, were other principal routes of travel.

Travelers complained constantly about the condition of all of these highways. Built and maintained by local labor, supervised by the overseers of roads in each township, the roads were ungraded, badly drained, and unsurfaced. Often they became quagmires in the spring, and their frozen ruts in winter were a constant menace to both man and beast. At each watercourse, travelers had to submit to vexatious delays while waiting for ferriage or, in some places, risk fording the stream. They faced, in addition, the unexaggerated torments inflicted by the formidable mosquitoes, which were inextricably identified with travel in New Jersey. By mid-century stages that were little more than springless farm wagons, with straight sides and a canvas covering under which passengers endured the discomforts of crude benches, traversed the province. Drawn by four or six horses, these jolting vehicles made it possible to go from New York to Philadelphia in three days. By 1775, when some refinements had been introduced and a few of the stages had been replaced by coaches, the trip could be made in two days, with a stop-over at Princeton.

The main highways were liberally dotted with taverns or inns, which provided indifferent accommodations for travelers. There were three or four hundred such hostelries in the province in 1775, many of them large establishments with spacious public rooms, several bedrooms, and ample stable facilities. Picturesque signboards, reminders of an age when literacy was far from universal, beckoned visitors to the King's Arms, the White Hart, the Red Lion, or the Bell. The innkeeper was frequently a citizen of considerable local prominence, and foreign travelers never ceased to be amazed—and disconcerted—by the unservile familiarity with which they were treated by their hosts. In addition to serving the weary traveler, the tavern was a social and political center of unrivaled importance. Public meetings, balls, elections, and celebrations were held there, and the taproom was constantly enlivened by the presence of local gentry assembled for gossip and frivolity. Probably no other institution played such a lively and vital role in colonial society.

COLONIAL ECONOMY

For most men who hazarded the role of colonists in a new land, the urge to better their economic condition was a dominating force. Whether he came from another colony or from across the Atlantic, the typical settler hoped to find in New Jersey enhanced opportunities to provide himself and his family with a satisfactory living. Attracted by the promise of good land at a reasonable price, by a favorable climate, and by a political environment that encouraged individual enterprise, he hoped to secure material rewards proportionate to his talents and his labor.

Many factors combined in New Jersey to afford the industrious man an unusual variety of economic pursuits. Here was no one-crop economy such as prevailed in some of the southern colonies or a distressing paucity of natural resources such as afflicted many New England communities. He might be a farmer, growing any one of a dozen main crops, a cattle-raiser, a lumberman, an iron miner, a merchant, a ship-owner, a craftsman, a fisherman, or a tavern-keeper. Frequently he combined several occupations. Variety, then, rather than homogeneity, characterized the economic scene.

By far the largest portion of the population was engaged in farming. The most common agricultural unit was around one hundred acres in size and could conveniently be operated by a single family, but there were abundant exceptions to this generalized picture. In Hunterdon and Sussex counties tenant farmers tilled the vast estates of absentee landowners. The Dutch in Somerset and Bergen, utilizing slave labor, were able to bring several hundred acres under cultivation on a single farm. In the southern counties, where cattle-raising was extensive, large farms were also common. Only in exceptional cases, however, was it feasible to rely heavily on paid laborers for large-scale farming operations, since hired hands were scarce in a country where good land was abundant.

The average farmer raised a great variety of crops, most of which were consumed within his own family. In many areas winter wheat was grown for the market, and it was the leading cash crop of the province. Rye, oats, buckwheat, barley, and flax, as well as common vegetables and such fruits as apples, peaches, cherries, and plums were standard crops, and most farms included some horses, cattle, pigs, sheep, and poultry. It was a rare yeoman who did not make a meal of his own buckwheat cakes, boiled cabbage, or salt pork; or dress in his own homespun wool or linen; or wear shoes cut from his own leather; or drink his own applejack and peach brandy.

The grazing of livestock, especially in the southern counties, was a profitable occupation. The cowboy—as he was called from an early date—was a familiar figure as he drove a large herd of cattle raised on the salt hay of Cape May or Cumberland to the markets in New York and Philadelphia. Hogs were slaughtered in large quantities and shipped in barrels to feed the populous, sugar-growing islands of the West Indies. Blooded horses, their pedigrees proudly advertised along with their stud fees in the newspapers, were imported from abroad to improve local breeds and thus make horse-raising a profitable enterprise. Bees, too, were utilized for economic ends, and within a two-year period ten barrels of beeswax were exported from Perth Amboy alone.

Agricultural practices were deplorably backward. By mid-century soil depletion was a serious problem in many sections. The intensive cultivation of corn early in the century, the practice of rotating fields rather than crops, and the failure to use fertilizers were all evidences of poor soil management. In part because land was seemingly inexhaustible and in part because of cultural factors, exploitation rather than cultivation best describes the colonial attitude toward land use. Equally imprudent methods were followed in handling livestock. Cattle were permitted to graze in unfenced fields; they remained outdoors the year round, and little attention was given to scientific breeding. The result was that they rapidly deteriorated in size and quality. Only in horse-raising and fruit-growing did most farmers apply the best knowledge available.

The life of the farmer in an era when labor-saving machinery did not exist was exceedingly laborious. Initially there was the staggering task of clearing the land, aided only by powerful teams of oxen. Then the soil was broken with an inefficient wooden plow drawn by horses. When harvest time arrived, grains would be cut with a hand scythe and threshed with techniques that had been employed since Biblical times. Because of the general scarcity of labor, it was customary for neighbors to join together to perform many functions. Barn-raisings, hog-butchering, harvests, and cattle drives were the occasions for "frolics" and "bees," and at such times sociability as well as industry reigned. While the men worked together from dawn to dusk, the women prepared repasts that would completely overwhelm modern appetites. At the end of the long day, the fiddle would be brought out, the cider jug would be passed around, and the evening would be devoted to dancing, courting, and friendly gossip. At such moments, an observation made in 1748 by Governor Belcher seemed especially apt: "Take this Province in the lump, it is the best country I have seen for men of middling fortunes, and for people who have to live by the sweat of their brows."

The outstanding industrial activity in the province was iron mining. As early as 1675 Lewis Morris had established an iron plantation in Tinton Manor (now Tinton Falls) in Monmouth County. In the succeeding half-century numerous rich magnetite and hematite mines were opened in Morris, Bergen, and Sussex. In Burlington and Gloucester counties bog-ore deposits in the beds of streams, resulting from the accumulation of certain iron salts drained from the soils of the surrounding area, were easily exploited. By the third quarter of the century, New Jersey rivaled Pennsylvania as a producer of pig iron and—despite British restrictions—was turning out quantities of manufactured iron articles.

The iron industry required tremendous capital resources, expert management, and technical skills—all of which were scarce in the new country. In addition to the mines themselves, forests were needed to supply the charcoal used in smelting the ore, limestone was required as a flux in the forges, and water power was essential to operate the bellows and other machinery. In addition, because the operation had to be carried on in a remote area, the ironmaster had to provide a self-sufficient community for his numerous workers.

The remarkable enterprise undertaken by Peter Hasenclever illustrates both the scope of the iron industry and the inherent difficulties that confronted the ironmaster. Hasenclever was a German instrumental in organizing the American Iron Company, a London syndicate with large financial resources. He came to America in 1764 and rapidly acquired several iron properties at Ringwood, Long Pond, and Charlottenburg. Then, within a year, he imported over five hundred persons from Germany to staff his installations. By 1766 he had four furnaces and seven forges in operation and was producing around sixty tons of pig iron a week. The Ringwood plantation, where Hasenclever lived in manorial grandeur, had one furnace, four forges, coalhouses, gristmills, sawmills, dwelling houses, and a millpond. Thousands of acres of nearby timberland were cut over and converted to charcoal. After spending some £55,000 on his vast, integrated industrial project, Hasenclever was unable to make of it a financial success, and by 1770 he had returned to England bankrupt.

In South Jersey, Charles Read of Burlington, holder of high political offices and an energetic speculator, joined with several associates to attempt a large-scale exploitation of bog-ore resources. He acquired four separate tracts and erected iron works at Taunton (Taunton Lake), Etna (Medford Lakes), Atsion, and Batsto between 1765 and 1770. Within a few years his enterprises brought about his financial collapse. Read left the colony, and other men took over the operation of individual works. During the Revolution, these establishments, together with those in

Bergen and Morris, played an important role in supplying the American Army. Other major iron centers were at Andover, Oxford, Mount Hope (Rockaway), Union (near High Bridge), Hibernia, and Speedwell (Morristown).

Commercial activities, usually conducted on a small scale, were carried on from many ports in the province. By far the greater part of New Jersey's exports were sent to New York, Philadelphia, and Rhode Island, from which places they might be shipped to the southern colonies, to the West Indies, or overseas. There were a few local ships engaged in direct trade with the West Indies, the Azores, and Madeira, but only in rare instances did a ship sail directly from New Jersey to England or the Continent. Small sloops, laden with wheat, flour, corn, boards, shingles, beef, pork, and horses set out from the numerous rivers and creeks that laced the perimeter of the province, bound for the nearby markets. Because of the great dispersion of commercial activity, which was largely the result of geographical factors, there were few large merchants of the type found in New York or Philadelphia, and merchants as a class were not so powerful or influential as in the neighboring colonies.

Lumbering and fishing offered a livelihood to many men. Woodchoppers and charcoal burners were employed in large numbers to serve the iron industry. Sawmills in all sections of the province turned out lumber in great quantities, much of it for export. Barrel staves, to be used in making hogsheads in the West Indies, were an important commodity. From the swamps of south Jersey ancient white cedars, three feet and more in diameter, were dug up—or "mined"—and converted into shingles whose wearing qualities made them highly desirable. Along the seacoast, and especially in Cape May, fisheries were a source of wealth. Throughout the eighteenth century, whaling was carried on by hardy and venturesome Jerseymen.

Colonial society was served by a host of skilled craftsmen, whose specialized abilities were highly regarded by an age that knew neither the machine nor mass production. Blacksmiths, farriers, wheelwrights, carpenters, millers, shoemakers, printers, masons, cabinetmakers, weavers, tanners and bakers—each serving a small area—became increasingly prominent as the economy matured. The storekeeper, whose stock of calicoes, silks, and bombazines tempted the local farmers' wives to unseemly extravagance and whose supplies of tea, coffee, spices, and sweetmeats injected a note of luxury into drab colonial menus, was able to offer his customers an astonishing variety of goods, usually in exchange for produce. Whereas in the seventeenth century each man had supplied most of his own wants, by the end of the eighteenth century economic specialization was far advanced; the pattern of society had become complex, and interdependence—rather than independence—characterized the relationship of each man with his fellows.

The State of Religion

Religious factors had played a prominent role in the early settlement of New Jersey. The promise of religious freedom offered by the proprietors and repeated under the royal regime influenced many groups strongly in their choice of New Jersey as a home. The Quaker pioneers in West Jersey, the transplanted Congregationalists of Newark, the once-persecuted Baptists of Piscataway and Middletown, and the Scottish Covenanters—to cite the outstanding examples—had sought above all a place where they might worship freely in accordance with their personal convictions. One of their most immediate concerns after their arrival here was to build a church and secure a pastor.

Within a generation or two, however, there was a marked decline in religious fervor. Many denominations experienced great difficulties in adjusting to the frontier environment. A dispersed population, struggling to obtain economic security, lacking educational facilities, and divided into numerous separate sects, could not readily establish strong religious institutions. In turn, because the churches were often feebly supported and poorly staffed, general religious interest dwindled. Although the

"Great Awakening" in mid-century sought to rouse the colonists from their religious lethargy, the state of religion continued to be a serious source of concern to church leaders in subsequent decades.

There were some one hundred and eighty congregations in the province by the end of the colonial period. Of these, fifty were Presbyterian, forty were Quaker, thirty were Dutch Reformed, thirty were Baptist, twenty were Anglican, and the remainder included German Lutherans, Swedish Lutherans, and Methodists. With the exception of the Quakers, who had no ministers, and the Baptists, whose churches were adequately staffed, two or three churches were served by a single pastor. Outside the larger towns, there was rarely more than one church within convenient reach, with the result that many people had the choice of attending a church other than that with which they had always been affiliated or not attending any religious services. In some sections, people were visited by ministers of their own denomination only once a year, at which time marriages were solemnized and baptisms took place.

The Presbyterians were in many respects the strongest religious group in the province. With substantial congregations in the main towns from Newark to Trenton, and in other parts of the province as well, they represented a blending of early New England Puritanism and Scottish Calvinism. Devoted to the ideal of a well educated ministry, they drew many of their early pastors from New England and Scotland. The founding by the Reverend William Tennent of the famous Log College at Neshaminy, Pennsylvania, around 1726, and the subsequent establishment of the College of New Jersey (Princeton) in 1746 afforded local opportunities for ministerial candidates. At the time of the "Great Awakening," the church was deeply stirred, and internal conflict arose over both the role of revivalism and the manner in which ministers should be qualified. The result was a schism, in 1741, into "New Light" and "Old Light" factions. Many of the churches in the northern half of the province withdrew from the Philadelphia Synod, a conservative stronghold, and it was not until 1758 that this breach was healed.

The Dutch Reformed Church, whose origins in the province dated from the establishment of churches at Bergen in 1661 and at Hackensack in 1686, possessed an advantage in that its members dwelled together within well defined regions, particularly in the Raritan and Hackensack valleys. Moreover, it was a national church, appealing strongly to every Dutch descendant. Its greatest handicap lay in the requirement that ministerial candidates obtain their training in Holland. Obviously, the expense and hazards of a trip abroad were discouraging factors, and the church had considerable difficulties on this score. Eventually there emerged two parties in the church after 1737. The Coetus, or liberal party, favored greater ecclesiastical autonomy for the American churches and a locally trained clergy. These views were opposed by the conservative Conferentie faction. A serious rift occurred between the two parties in 1754, and was only partially healed by the efforts of the Reverend John Livingston in 1771.

The Anglicans, requiring candidates for holy orders to go to England for ordination, also found it impossible to provide sufficient ministers. The small number of communicants and their dispersion also presented problems. Even in Perth Amboy and Burlington, Anglican centers from earliest times, the congregations were small, and they frequently went for long periods without a resident pastor. Throughout the period, Anglican missionaries were supported in large part from England by the Society for the Propagation of the Gospel in Foreign Parts, which recognized the economic weakness of Anglicanism in those colonies where the Church was not established. Rarely, however, were there more than six or seven such missionaries to serve the entire province.

The Baptists, whose earliest churches in New Jersey had been established in Middletown, Piscataway, and Cohansey, readily adapted themselves to the American environment. According to each congregation a high degree of autonomy and not requiring elaborate training for ministerial candidates, they did not labor under the handicaps that hampered the growth of many other denominations. Although there was not a single Baptist church in any of the larger towns, a fact which is not easily explained, there were churches in all sections of the province and they were well supplied with settled pastors. Essentially a rural group made up of yeoman farmers, the Baptists furnished relatively few political leaders and engaged in no public controversies.

The Society of Friends continued throughout the eighteenth century to exert a distinctive influence in West Jersey. Lacking the peculiar fervor that had stamped them as religious radicals in the previous century, the Quakers manifested increasing concern with social problems and took leadership in many areas of humanitarian reform. Impelled by that saintly Friend, John Woolman, of Mount Holly, they came out firmly against slave holding in 1758, displayed a deep concern for the plight of the Indians, developed a system of education, and even began to withdraw from political activities because of their opposition to war and military preparations. More than any other denomination, they were to serve as the moral conscience for the new society.

In addition to the five major denominations, several other sects were represented in the province. The German population, which was settled chiefly in the upper Raritan, in Hunterdon, and Sussex, was inadequately served by a handful of German Reformed, German Lutheran, and Moravian pastors, who were called upon to visit several widely dispersed congregations in such centers as Amwell in Hunterdon County, New Germantown, Rockaway, Bedminster, and even Cohansey. Trinity Church at Raccoon Creek and struggling congregations at Penn's Neck (Churchtown) and Repaupo continued within the Swedish Lutheran Church as late as 1786, when Nicholas Collin, their last pastor, left the state. Methodism had barely gained a foothold by 1775. Despite the many preaching tours of Francis Asbury, there were well established societies only in Burlington and Trenton. Not until the nineteenth century were there any Roman

Catholic churches or Jewish synagogues in New Jersey.

The most significant religious movement of the century was the "Great Awakening," and few churches escaped its wide influence. The movement developed essentially as a reaction against the apathy, formalism, and lack of spirituality that characterized religion in the first decades of the century. It emphasized ardent evangelism and sought to make religion a stirring personal experience. One of its precursors in New Jersey was Theodorus Jacobus Frelinghuysen, who arrived in the Raritan valley in 1720 and was soon arousing controversy with his revivalist preaching among the Dutch congregations there. The great English Wesleyan evangelist, George Whitefield, attracted audiences of several thousand when he spoke in New Jersey in 1739 and left a powerful impression on this and subsequent visits. One of his ardent followers was Gilbert Tennent, pastor of the Presbyterian Church in New Brunswick, and Tennent soon emerged as one of the leaders of the "New Light" party.

As a result of the new religious currents set in motion by the "Great Awakening," both the Presbyterian and the Dutch Reformed Churches were divided into conservative and liberal factions. One of the consequences of the ferment was a heightened interest in education, which in turn led to the founding of numerous academies and two colleges: the College of New Jersey and Queen's College. The permanent effects of the revival in terms of expanded church memberships and deepened spiritual life have been questioned, but the movement did serve to arouse many congregations and denominations to an awareness of the problems with which they must somehow cope if the cause of religion was to flourish in the new land.

EDUCATION AND THE ARTS

The energy and the competence displayed by the colonial pioneers in transforming a virgin wilderness into a region of settled farms, in developing a stable political order, in creating essential social and religious institutions—all within the space of two or three generations—

was most impressive. Handicapped by primitive technological equipment but favored by an environment that held the promise of abundance and a cultural climate that emphasized freedom and opportunity for the individual, the colonists made extraordinary progress in building for themselves a way of life that reflected their deep and varied aspirations. It would almost have seemed that whatever man desired was obtainable in this wondrous new land where hope was far stronger than fear and courage vanquished despair. That the aspirations of the colonists extended far beyond providing themselves merely with the creature comforts is evidenced by their early interest in education, in cultural self-expression, and in the betterment of mankind through the reform of what they came to regard as social evils.

Concern for education was never entirely lacking in the province, although it was not until around the middle of the eighteenth century that economic and social conditions permitted the development of an educational system that extended beyond the level of the common school. Almost from the first years of their settlement, such towns as Newark, Woodbridge, and Piscataway—in part owing to their New England origins—had made provisions for a schoolhouse and a teacher. Other towns followed suit, and by 1700 the essential features of the township system of common schools had been generally adopted, especially in East Jersey. Outside of the principal towns, it was the practice for parents to join together in hiring a schoolmaster, who, in such rude quarters as might be available, would give instruction in the three R's. In West Jersey educational activities lagged until the eve of the Revolution when the Quakers, spurred by such farsighted leaders as John Woolman and Anthony Benezet, set themselves the goal of establishing schools in conjunction with each meeting. Because of the chronic shortage of teachers, most of these schools functioned only intermittently, and the pupils achieved little more than basic literacy.

In time, the need for schools to provide the classical type of education that would qualify students for college and for entry into the learned professions resulted in the founding of numerous grammar schools and academies. The Presbyterians were especially active in this field, and many classes started by ministers in their own studies for boys of the neighborhood grew into flourishing schools. In the third quarter of the century more than a dozen such schools came into existence, of which the ones in Newark, Elizabeth, New Brunswick, Princeton, Hackensack, Freehold, and Hopewell were most prominent and successful. Offering usually a four-year course with emphasis on the classics, science, and mathematics, they were essentially democratic in their appeal and attracted students from many different segments of colonial society.

New Jersey was unique among the colonies in that it alone had two colleges. The College of New Jersey (Princeton University) owed its origin largely to the desire of certain "New Light" Presbyterian leaders to provide proper education for ministers, although from the first the college was not under the control of the Church nor was its purpose restricted to training ministers. Chartered in 1746, the school was in a feeble condition for a decade, during which time it moved from Elizabeth to Newark. The enthusiastic patronage of Governor Jonathan Belcher brought many benefits to the struggling institution, and when it moved to Princeton in 1756 to occupy the yet-unfinished Nassau Hall, its future seemed assured. With the arrival of the Reverend John Witherspoon from Scotland in 1768 to assume the presidency, the college secured a remarkable leader who greatly strengthened the faculty, attracted promising students from many colonies, reformed the system of instruction and—not the least of his accomplishments—made Princeton a nursery of future leaders of the Whig cause.

Queen's College (Rutgers University) was chartered in 1766 to give instruction in "the learned languages and other branches of useful knowledge." Like Princeton, it was not a sectarian institution, but its founders were chiefly men of the liberal party of the Dutch Reformed Church who were anxious to establish an institution where candidates for the ministry could be educated.

AULA NASSOVICA.

Nassau Hall, Princeton University

Built in 1756, Nassau Hall served as the first meeting place of the state legislature in August, 1776, and of the Continental Congress, June-November, 1783.

Courtesy of The New York Historical Society, New York City

After some competition between Hackensack and New Brunswick, the trustees decided to locate the college at the latter town, and classes began in 1771 with a single tutor, Frederick Frelinghuysen, in charge. The student body numbered scarcely more than a score when the Revolution began, and soon the activities of the college were interrupted by the British occupation of the city. After the war regular classes were resumed in New Brunswick, but the institution had a precarious existence until 1825, when its name was changed to Rutgers College and a new and promising era was inaugurated.

Many young men from New Jersey went outside the province for their education, to the colonial colleges in New England, New York, or Philadelphia, and in rare instances to the old universities in England. Most of those who wished to enter the two favorite secular professions—law and medicine—received their training as apprentices to practitioners. Lawyers were "a numerous breed," and they were frequently under attack for charging excessive fees. Members of the medical profession were few. When the New Jersey Medical Society was organized in July, 1766, it had 14 members; a decade later there were 26, a few of whom had received formal training at the medical school in Philadelphia or abroad.

Opportunities for self-education were limited, for there were no newspapers published in New Jersey prior to the Revolution, books were expensive and relatively rare, and there was but one public library of consequence, founded in 1752 in Burlington. The average family owned a Bible, some religious tracts or sermons, and perhaps one or two volumes on practical subjects. Many men of wealth and culture, however, built up libraries of several hundred volumes, and it was decidedly fashionable to be able to discourse familiarly about the latest London works in science, politics, and theology. A cultivated Englishman visiting the province in 1775 would not have found himself lacking the company of men of refined tastes and broad learning.

Practical concern absorbed most of the energies of

those who were engaged in building the new society, but artistic expression was not entirely neglected. John Watson, one of the earliest painters in the colonies, had established himself at Perth Amboy by 1714, built up a remarkable art collection made up of his own works and many imported from Europe, and painted some fine portraits of prominent men. Patience Wright, who came from a family distinguished for artistic talents in Burlington County, did outstanding work in wax sculpture and had many of her pieces exhibited in London. Other artists and "limners," working in oil or pastel, eked out a living by doing portraits of anyone who could afford their modest fees.

Musical activities were confined chiefly to church singing and private instrumental groups, but two men associated with New Jersey achieved distinction as the earliest colonial composers. Francis Hopkinson, who signed the Declaration of Independence for New Jersey and who resided for some years in Bordentown, was a talented amateur, composing songs, oratorios, and selections for the harpsichord. His first song, "My Days Have Been So Wondrous Free," was written in 1759, and a collection of his psalm tunes was published in 1763. James Lyon composed an ode for his commencement at the College of New Jersey in 1759 and later published many songs and a book for teaching singing.

In the field of literary endeavor, most writing took the form of sermons, religious tracts, and political pamphlets. Philip Freneau had barely launched a career that was to win him the title of "Poet of the Revolution" and a high rank among early American poets. The Quaker John Woolman had written the moving *Journal* that was to stand as one of the great records of a deeply spiritual life. Samuel Smith, the cultivated and learned Quaker from Burlington, published his *History of the Colony of Nova-Caesaria, or New Jersey* in 1765, which commands respect even today. One of the most curious literary efforts was the work of Joseph Morgan, Presbyterian minister at Freehold. His *History of the Kingdom of Bassa-*

ruah, published in 1715, was a complex religious allegory in the style of Bunyan and one of the first examples of prose fiction produced in America.

Although evidences of formal interest in the arts was not lacking in colonial New Jersey, the principal outlet for artistic expression was unquestionably in the crafts. The skilled men, most of them now quite unknown to us, who produced beautiful pieces of silverware, furniture, glassware, or ironwork were artists no less than they were craftsmen. The finely proportioned houses and the simple, dignified churches as well as the cleverly designed quilts and the intricately worked samplers that have survived as a cultural heritage from that early period testify to the extraordinary sense of taste possessed by the colonial artisans.

HUMANITARIAN CONCERNS

The new society that developed in colonial New Jersey was not free from imperfections, and—particularly after the middle of the eighteenth century—voices of protest were raised against many social evils. Strong-willed men and women, motivated most frequently by religious feelings of charity and humanitarianism, dedicated themselves to the work of reform. Most prominent in these movements were the Quakers, although as the years passed they won many allies among the members of other denominations. In a sense, the stirrings of social criticism were evidence of the increasing maturity of colonial society. The old order had reached a point where criticism was both possible and tolerable.

One of the unfortunate groups that aroused humanitarian concern was the Indians. Ever since the arrival of the English, relations between the whites and the aborigines had been friendly. But as the settled area within the colony expanded, the Indians yielded their lands to the proprietary purchasers and moved out of New Jersey. Those who did remain lived in small clan-groups, their traditional way of life disrupted by the presence of their white neighbors and their bodies prey to the white man's diseases. Living apart and for the most part ignored, their sad lot attracted little notice until around 1740, when a group of Presbyterian ministers in New Jersey and New York solicited and received from Scotland funds for the support of missionary activities among the Indians. As a result of this action, the Reverend David Brainerd, a dedicated young graduate of Yale, began his work with the Indians of New Jersey.

After preaching for a time along the upper Delaware, Brainerd moved to Crosswicks in 1745 and a year later to Cranbury, where he sought to bring to the small band of natives who followed him the blessings of his own strong faith. Worn out by his labors, David Brainerd died in 1747, but his brother, John, continued the work until he moved to Newark in 1755. In the meantime, interest had been kindled in the idea of establishing an adequate reservation within the province where the two or three hundred remaining aborigines might find a secure haven. A group of Quakers organized "The New Jersey Association for Helping the Indians" to promote that objective. Finally, in 1758, following the surrender by the Indians of their remaining land claims south of the Raritan, the provincial legislature purchased a tract of some three thousand acres near present-day Indian Mills in Burlington County.

A settlement—appropriately named Brotherton—was started and several houses and a church were built. John Brainerd became superintendent of the reservation, and over a hundred Lenapes were attracted to the project. Despite the self-sacrificing labors of Brainerd and the friendly support of the government, the enterprise did not prosper. By 1774 there were no more than sixty Indians remaining at Brotherton, and by 1801 the last Lenape had departed to northern New York. The effort to assist the Indians and to Christianize them must be judged a failure, but the motives that inspired the effort and especially the devotion shown by Brainerd and his supporters command respect and admiration.

The existence of the institution of slavery similarly aroused concern. It is estimated that in 1775 nearly one-twelfth of New Jersey's population of 115,000 was made up of Negroes, all but a small number of whom were slaves. Only New York, among the northern states, had a larger number of slaves. From all accounts, these unfortunate people were treated as well as their condition permitted, but they had no civil rights and were subjected to special legal codes. In times of public hysteria, such as that following the alleged Negro plot of 1741 in New York, suspected slaves were burned at the stake in Hackensack and Elizabeth. Efforts to curtail the importation of slaves into the province by imposing import duties on them met with no success until 1767. The Quakers, who came out officially in opposition to slaveholding in 1758, agitated for legislation that would encourage individual owners to manumit their slaves and for a complete ban on further importations, but these goals were not achieved until after the Revolution.

The exceedingly harsh criminal code of the time was another vestige of the inhumanity of earlier times and customs. Severe punishments were prescribed for most offenses in accordance with a stern tradition. Punishment took the form of whipping, cropping, branding, and hanging. Jails, which had been erected at an early date in each county, were merely places of detention; they housed only those criminal offenders awaiting trial or punishment. Their chief occupants were usually debtors, who were obliged to remain in custody until their debts had been paid or until one of the periodic acts for the relief of debtors had been passed by the legislature. On the whole, these brutal conditions were tolerated, except by the Quakers.

Colonial society was not without its harsh and inhuman features, but such elements represented an inheritance from the past. Over the years, as the brutalizing influence of the struggle for survival in a new environment receded, men sought to provide themselves with those benefits of civilization that make life, not merely bearable, but pleasant and edifying.

It was apparent by the third quarter of the century that a new society had emerged from the wilderness, different from its sources in the Old World. Made up of people of diverse religious and national origins, it had failed to reproduce many of those institutions that in Europe inhibited freedom. Instead, by stressing individual enterprise and political responsibility, it promised a greater measure of freedom for all men than any previous society in history. Having arrived at this condition, it was now to be confronted with those decisions that led ultimately to independence and nationhood.

VI

THE MOVEMENT
FOR INDEPENDENCE

In the decade following the French and Indian War
profound changes took place in the relationships between Great Britain and her American colonies. The
long era of indifference and laxity came to an abrupt
end. Soon the colonists were confronted with a series of
enactments that tightened British control over commerce,
money, manufacturing, fur trading, western lands, Indian relations, and defense. Even more drastic, the colonies were asked to pay taxes levied by Parliament. From
the British point of view these policies were necessary
and proper. The great war just ended had been extremely costly, and the problem of financing the administration of a far-flung empire could be solved only if the
colonies bore their fair share of the burden. Moreover,
it seemed that many general matters affecting the American colonies collectively—such as defense, trade regulation, and currency—could be dealt with effectively only
by the central legislative body of the empire, which was
Parliament.

This reorganization of the imperial structure meant,
in brief, that the individual colonies were going to lose a
large degree of the freedom they had long enjoyed in
managing their own affairs. Not all colonies were uniformly affected by the new controls. Those, like Virginia,
that had claims to vast territories in the west were hurt
by the restrictive land policies. Others with extensive
commercial interests, like Massachusetts, resented the

restraints on trade due to enforcement of the mercantile system. All of the colonies, however, found a common cause for grievance in the imposition of taxes by Parliament, and in time all came to question the authority of Parliament to legislate on American affairs. These issues gave rise to a great constitutional debate and to the mobilization of forces of resistance to what were regarded as unjust and illegal measures. Eventually, debate was succeeded by violence, and the colonists embarked upon a battle for their rights, as they understood them. The next step was to transform a war for their "rights as Englishmen" into a war for independence.

STIRRINGS OF DISCONTENT

The people of New Jersey, as they greeted with enthusiasm the victorious conclusion of the French and Indian War, were fervent in their loyalty to the Crown and had no thoughts that the years ahead would be full of conflict with the mother country. Although saddled with a large debt and heavy taxes, the province welcomed its new governor, William Franklin, early in 1763 with every manifestation of good will. Destined to be the last royal governor of the province, this accomplished son of the distinguished philosopher and statesman, Benjamin Franklin, had every reason to anticipate a successful administration. As a youth in Pennsylvania he had won a captaincy in King George's War, after which he had served in minor administrative posts. He had accompanied his father to England in 1756, studied law, and been admitted to the bar. His personal charm and his recognized abilities—as well as his father's position —brought him to the attention of the powerful Earl of Bute, through whose influence he was appointed to the governorship. Only thirty-two years old, he soon displayed a rare gift for dealing with the various political factions in the province, at the same time zealously protecting the prerogatives of the Crown.

For some two years after his arrival public affairs proceeded smoothly in New Jersey. Although signs of restiveness were already apparent in other colonies whose

Governor William Franklin

The son of Benjamin Franklin and royal governor of New Jersey from 1763 to 1776, William Franklin remained zealously loyal to the Crown. He went to England in 1782 and remained there until his death in 1813.

commercial or territorial interests were being adversely affected by the new British policies, New Jersey—having little commerce and no western land claims—was not aroused. But this complacency was shattered when news arrived that Parliament in March, 1765, had passed the Stamp Act.

This measure, which was intended to raise money to finance the defense of the colonies, required the purchase of stamps that were to be affixed to legal documents, bills of lading, liquor licenses, newspapers, almanacs, and other items. Never before had Parliament attempted to levy a direct tax on the colonies. Throughout America there was general recognition of the seriousness of this innovation. For centuries it had been understood that Englishmen could be taxed only by their own representatives. This right had been clearly affirmed in the first charters of New Jersey and other colonies. Now, it seemed this right was being violated.

New Jersey's initial reaction to the Stamp Act was relatively mild. When the assembly received a circular letter in June, 1765, from Massachusetts calling for an intercolonial meeting, it declined to send representatives and suggested that moderation rather than hasty action was called for. But as the summer wore on, according to Governor Franklin, "violent papers" were sent into New Jersey from the neighboring colonies to stir up popular sentiment. Late in September the lawyers of the province met in Perth Amboy and decided not to buy the hated stamps or do any legal business. This example soon spread to other colonies. On September 21 there appeared *The Constitutional Courant,* published at the press of James Parker in Woodbridge. Containing strong denunciation of Parliament, this "first newspaper" in New Jersey did not survive beyond the initial number, but it created a momentary sensation.

As public indignation mounted, the speaker of the assembly, Robert Ogden, belatedly called the members of that body to meet in Perth Amboy early in October to select representatives to attend the Stamp Act Congress in New York City. Held without the sanction of the governor, this extra-legal session chose Ogden, Hendrick Fisher, and Joseph Borden as its delegates. The Congress, which was attended by twenty-eight delegates from nine colonies, adopted a set of resolutions condemning taxation without representation and petitioning the King and Parliament to repeal the Stamp Act. Robert Ogden refused to assent to the resolutions, arguing that individual protests by each colony would be more effective than the joint appeal. For this stand he was strongly criticized and was burned in effigy in several New Jersey towns. Shortly thereafter he resigned his seat in the assembly.

When the New Jersey legislature met in November, 1765, it heard a report from its delegates to the Stamp Act Congress. The assembly gave unanimous approval to the actions of the Congress and endorsed a set of resolutions that forcefully and clearly set forth the basic issues. The key sections declared:

That it is inseparably essential to the freedom of a people, and the undoubted right of Englishmen, that no taxes be imposed on them but with their own consent given personally, or by their representatives.

That the people of this colony are not, and from their remote situation cannot be represented in the parliament of Great-Britain, and if the principle of taxing the colonies without their own consent should be adopted, the people here would be subjected to the taxation of two legislatures; a grievance unprecedented, and not to be thought of without the greatest anxiety.

That the only representatives of the people of this colony are persons chosen by themselves, and that no taxes ever have been, or can be imposed on them, agreeable to the constitution of this province, granted and confirmed by his Majesty's most gracious predecessors, but by their own legislature.

Virtually all segments of colonial society were in agreement with these sentiments.

While the constitutional debate was proceeding, popular agitation was producing an inflamed opinion that threatened to end in acts of violence. In the early stages of the controversy ardent spirits banded together in an organization known as the Sons of Liberty. At its peak this aggressive body numbered several thousand members in various parts of the province, with a hierarchy of committees to maintain correspondence among themselves and with other colonies. In addition to holding protest meetings at which strongly-worded declarations were adopted, the Sons of Liberty took it upon themselves to see that the Stamp Act would not be put into effect.

When it seemed that the lawyers of the province might be weakening in their resistance to the measure, they were waited upon by several hundred Sons of Liberty at a general meeting in New Brunswick and were induced to give assurances of their steadfastness. Similarly, when some doubts arose as to whether William Coxe, who had been appointed Stamp Agent for New Jersey, had indeed resigned his post, a delegation of Sons visited him and received the necessary guarantees. So tense was the situation that Governor Franklin prudently arranged to have the stamps that were destined for New Jersey kept aboard a warship in New York harbor. To have brought them into the colony might have precipitated violence.

The resistance put up by the colonies was effective. Impressed by the vigor of the opposition and by the economic losses suffered by English merchants as a result of the decline in American trade, Parliament repealed the Stamp Act in March, 1766. Great was the rejoicing in New Jersey, where huge public meetings were held to express affection for the King as well as to hail the triumph of the colonial cause. But the contest was far from over, for Parliament insisted explicitly that, despite its repeal of the Stamp Act it nevertheless had the right to legislate for the colonies in all matters, including taxation.

That the colonial rejoicing had been premature became clear when word arrived in 1767 that Parliament had enacted the Townshend Duties taxing imports of glass, paper, paint, and tea. It was intended that the revenue so raised would be used to pay the salaries of colonial officials, thus making them independent of the assembly. Massachusetts again led the protest against this new "unconstitutional tax," and called for the support of other colonies in petitioning the King and in boycotting English goods. The New Jersey assembly in May, 1768, heeded this plea, and in secret session drew up a petition that recited their ancient "Rights and Liberties," one of which was exemption from taxes except those imposed by their own representatives. Once again there were public meetings to condemn the Parliamentary exactions. Trade dwindled as conscientious Whigs refused to buy British products. The graduating class at Princeton made a point of dressing in clothes of American manufacture exclusively. The British ministry, now led by Lord North, at last recognized defeat, and in April, 1770, all the duties except that on tea were repealed. Although this action quieted colonial opposition, objection in principle to the tea tax continued, and abstinence from the use of this popular beverage became the mark of the true patriot.

Meanwhile, other issues arose to agitate the public scene. When New Jersey was required by the Mutiny Act of 1765 to furnish certain supplies for British troops quartered in the several barracks in the province, many there were who regarded this measure as no more than a disguised tax. Year after year, there was wrangling between the governor and the assembly over the manner in which the barracks should be supplied, and the lawmakers stubbornly refused to comply exactly with the requirements laid down by Parliament.

Another source of constant irritation was the refusal of the home authorities to approve a new loan-office measure. With a steady deflation producing hard times and economic stringency, some solution to the province's currency problem was urgently needed. Not until 1774 was the plea for a loan office granted, and by then it was too late.

A long-drawn-out quarrel between Governor Franklin and the assembly over the status of Stephen Skinner,

Treasurer of East Jersey, added to the troubles of the times. When the East Jersey treasury was mysteriously robbed of nearly £8000 in 1768, the assembly called for Skinner's resignation. Franklin, insisting that the treasurer was removable only by the governor, refused to yield to their pressure. This controversy dragged on until 1774, when Skinner finally resigned.

Throughout these years, it should be stressed, there was a high degree of unanimity within the province in opposition to what were regarded as the unconstitutional exactions of the British Parliament. Those who were later to become ardent Tories as well as those who were to lead the patriot cause joined in protesting against the trend of British policy. At the same time, no voice was raised in favor of independence, and the King remained as ever an object of loyal devotion.

The Road to Rebellion

The opposition to British policies took on a new character following the Boston Tea Party and its immediate consequences. Within little more than a year there emerged in each colony organizations whose initial purpose was to maintain the rights of the people in the face of Parliamentary "tyranny." But soon these organizations were exercising governmental functions as, by degrees, they were transformed into instruments of rebellion. Events in New Jersey in the exciting period between the Tea Party and the Declaration of Independence illustrate the manner in which a revolution is made.

It was in December, 1773, that Sam Adams' band of "Indians" dumped the tea of the East India Company into Boston harbor. This incident shifted the controversy between Britain and the colonies from the relatively orderly area of constitutional debate to the arena of violent, direct action. Shocked and even enraged by this dramatic evidence of rebelliousness, Britain responded with a series of harsh, punitive measures known as the Intolerable Acts. Both sides had now stepped over the line of reasonableness, and each party could point intemperately to the unjust measures of its antagonist.

Once again, as they had done during the agitation against the Stamp Act and the Townshend Duties, the colonies prepared for joint resistance. In anticipation of what lay ahead Virginia proposed that each colony appoint a committee of correspondence, so that mutual consultation might be facilitated. The New Jersey assembly created a Committee of Correspondence on February 8, 1774, and placed at its head James Kinsey, Quaker lawyer of Burlington, long an outstanding advocate of colonial rights. For several months Kinsey was to be the most active figure in mobilizing the forces of resistance in New Jersey, although ultimately he balked at the decision for independence and remained a "neutral" throughout the war. After news of the Intolerable Acts reached New Jersey, Kinsey tried without success to induce the governor to convene the legislature. At the same time he sought to arouse other leading men in the province to the importance of the issues raised by the most recent British actions.

As the seriousness of the situation became increasingly apparent, public meetings were held in several counties during June and July, 1774, to organize county Committees of Correspondence. These bodies in the months ahead were to be centers of the resistance movement. The next important step came on July 21, when 72 members of the county committees met in convention in New Brunswick. With Stephen Crane, former speaker of the assembly from Essex presiding, this body made several historic decisions during its three-day session.

In a series of resolutions the Convention first of all expressed loyalty to the King and detestation of "all thoughts of independence." But it went on to condemn the stand taken by Parliament—especially with regard to taxation—and to propose that the colonies should agree not to import or consume British products, and to approve the holding of an intercolonial congress. Five delegates—James Kinsey, William Livingston, John De Hart, Stephen Crane, and Richard Smith—were appointed to attend the first Continental Congress, which was to convene in Philadelphia in September. Thus, within a few months, there was brought into being an extra-legal political structure extending from the county level up to the intercolonial level, and the royal officials in America felt themselves powerless to intervene in the course of affairs.

The Continental Congress, in addition to restating colonial grievances and petitioning for relief, took concrete measures to strengthen colonial resistance. A non-importation, non-exportation agreement was formulated, with a view to putting economic pressure on Britain. For the enforcement of this agreement, an "Association" was created to which all loyal patriots gave their support. Elected committees in each county and town assumed the task of making the boycott effective. When these proposals had been carried out in New Jersey, the populace was in effect subject to two governments, one official and the other extra-legal. Further sanction was given to these arrangements in January, 1775, when the assembly, without a dissenting note, gave its approval to the actions of the Continental Congress and reappointed the same five delegates to attend the second Congress when it might be convened.

Down to this point the American cause enjoyed widespread and even enthusiastic support in New Jersey. Dissident voices were few. But as the number of committees multiplied and set about their work, people were really forced to make decisions and take sides. Some, either through timidity or through a sincere reluctance to disturb ancient bonds, were loath to join the Association or submit to dictation from irregular bodies. Others were alarmed as they saw radical men coming to the fore, and their conservative tendencies were aroused. By April, 1775, when the battles of Lexington and Concord signalized the start of armed rebellion, internal divisions were becoming pronounced.

When the New Jersey Committee of Correspondence learned that hostilities had begun, it called upon the counties to elect delegates to what has become known as the first Provincial Congress. Elected in various ways, the 87 members of the Provincial Congress convened in

Trenton on May 23, and—with short adjournments—
remained in session until September.

Recognizing that the colony must prepare to defend
itself by force of arms, the Congress provided for the
creation of an elaborate militia system embracing men
between the ages of sixteen and fifty. To finance defense
preparations a tax of £10,000 was levied, with assessment
and collection of the tax put in the hands of the local
committees. Having gone this far in the exercise of the
major powers of government, the Congress placed the
revolutionary organization on a regular basis by providing for a system of annual elections for members of the
Provincial Congress, county committees, and township
committees. In effect, a full-fledged state within a state
had come into being.

The structure of royal government in New Jersey
still remained intact. Governor Franklin convened the
legislature in May in the hope that it would give favorable consideration to the so-called Conciliatory Resolves
of Lord North. But the assembly found the proposals
unacceptable and declined to make any answer to them
until the second Continental Congress should act. The
final meeting of the old assembly was held in November,
1775. The governor addressed the two houses briefly and
without passion on the "unhappy situation of public affairs." After advising them that the King intended to use
military force to put down the rebellion, he asked them
to tell him candidly whether his own person was in danger and whether independence was the objective in view.

After several days, the assembly drew up a reply to
the governor's message. Expressing surprise that Franklin should think himself in danger, they urged him not
to leave the province. Further, they asserted that they
knew of "no sentiments of independency that are by
men of consequence, openly avowed" and stated their
"detestation" of such sentiments. Indeed, they instructed their delegates to the Continental Congress "not
to give their assent to, but utterly to reject any proposi-
tions, if such should be made, that may separate this
Colony from the Mother Country, or change the form

of Government thereof." After voting the usual support bill for the salaries of government officials, the legislature adjourned in December, never to meet again.

Meanwhile, the second Provincial Congress, elected in September, 1775, was taking over the actual government of the province. The militia system was strengthened; the issuance of £50,000 in bills of credit was authorized; arrangements were made for the purchase of guns, ammunition, blankets, and other military supplies. In response to an appeal from the Continental Congress in Philadelphia three battalions of infantry were raised for the Continental service. The initial commanders of these troops—each with the rank of colonel—were William Alexander (Lord Stirling), William Maxwell, and Elias Dayton, all of whom were to serve loyally and with distinction throughout the war.

In February, 1776, as the result of numerous complaints, a new election ordinance was approved. Formerly, only those who owned real estate could vote. Now anyone whose property—real or personal—was worth £50 was eligible to vote. In that it represented the overthrow of the old notion that only landowners should enjoy full political privileges, this act was one of the first fruits of the revolutionary upheaval.

Much of the time of the Congress was of necessity taken up with disputes over the naming of military officers and with various problems created by men who chose to flout the authority of the Provincial Congress. Jail sentences and stiff fines were meted out to numerous individuals who declined to support the Association, and with each passing week it became more apparent that the population was dividing into two opposing parties as independence loomed ahead.

When elections were held for the third Provincial Congress on May 28, 1776, the time for decision was at hand. For more than a year, colonial forces had been fighting against the soldiers of George III. Thomas Paine had published his inflammatory *Common Sense,* advocating renunciation of all allegiance to the King. No firm basis for compromising the differences between the two adversaries could be put forth. Above all, what had originated as a somewhat spontaneous resistance-movement had now taken on all the attributes of a functioning revolutionary government. In Philadelphia the Continental delegates voted on May 15 to advise each colony to draft state constitutions. Independence was at last being openly discussed and advocated as the only real alternative for America.

All these facts were evident to the citizens of New Jersey who voted in May for the new Provincial Congress. When that body convened at Burlington on June 10, 1776, it was no secret that a majority of its members were prepared to take the final step. They met at a time of great tension and excitement. In June the British forces under Lord Howe were preparing to invade New York and launch a vigorous campaign that would imperil the security of New Jersey. Heartened by the strength at last displayed by England, hundreds of men in all sections of the province came out in open opposition to the rebel party. "Disaffected persons," in some places engaged in organized defiance of the Congress. Many men who had taken prominent roles in the early stages of the struggle for the rights of the colonies now withdrew or came out on the Loyalist side. In certain counties large numbers of officers in the militia resigned their commissions. Henceforth, there was to be a civil war within New Jersey as well as a revolt against the mother country.

In the midst of these many trials the Congress courageously took actions that seemed necessary. On June 16 it was ordered that Governor Franklin—who had been under close surveillance for some weeks—should be taken into custody. He was brought to Burlington a few days later and given a hearing before the Congress, but he stoutly refused to recognize the authority of the body and would answer no questions. On June 25, in obedience to the directions of the Continental Congress, he was sent off to Connecticut, where he remained a prisoner until he was exchanged in 1778. He then became for a time the embittered head of the Board of Associated Loyalists in New York City. In 1782 he went to

England, living there on a pension from the British government until his death in 1813.

The Provincial Congress next devoted its attention to the matter of independence. On June 21 it resolved to draft a new constitution. On the following day it chose an entirely new set of delegates to the Continental Congress, for those who had been representing the province had either resigned or had manifested reluctance to sever completely the ties with England. Those chosen to go to Philadelphia were Richard Stockton of Princeton, an outstanding lawyer and former member of the governor's council; John Hart, a Hopewell farmer; Francis Hopkinson of Bordentown, also a former member of the council; Abraham Clark of Elizabeth, a farmer and surveyor who had been sheriff of Essex; and Dr. John Witherspoon, the fiery president of the College of New Jersey. They were instructed to vote for a declaration of independence and for a union of the colonies to provide for the common defense. All of these patriots approved and signed the historic document that marked the birth of a new nation.

The next task was to create a frame of government to replace that which was being discarded. There was little time for mature deliberation. The military situation was becoming increasingly critical, with British invasion an imminent possibility. A functioning government based on law was urgently needed to cope with the problems of the day. Accordingly, a ten-man committee under the chairmanship of Jacob Green, Presbyterian minister from Morris County, was appointed on June 24. Working with great haste, the committee returned a draft two days later, which was adopted, after a few days of debate, on July 2.

Thus on the same day that the Continental Congress was voting its approval of independence, New Jersey took the decisive action in launching its career as a state. The Provincial Congress continued in session until August 21, and a week later the new legislature of the state convened at Princeton. The old order had passed, a new one was beginning.

Richard Stockton

An eminent lawyer and member of the royal governor's council, Stockton was the most prominent New Jersey signer of the Declaration of Independence. His home was Morven, now the official residence of New Jersey's governor.

Courtesy of Princeton University

How did it happen that New Jersey, where scarcely a murmur of independence was to be heard in 1774, found itself in 1776 engaged in a war to defend its newly asserted freedom? Great weight, of course, must be given to the fact that the Revolution was an intercolonial movement and New Jersey's course was very strongly influenced by what was taking place throughout the colonies. In a sense New Jersey was carried along on the main tide; it did not take an aggressive position of leadership, as did Massachusetts and Virginia.

But that is not the whole explanation. New Jersey had its own grievances, which initially served to stimulate widespread resistance to British policies. Even so-called conservatives participated in organizing for the protection of American rights. With their long background of political experience in the techniques of self-government the people displayed rare ability in setting up committees, conventions, and congresses to give depth and structure to their opposition. Then, when peaceful measures failed and hostilities began in April, 1775, the movement took on a new aspect. Men had to take sides. They had to decide whether to stand with England, regardless of grievances, or take up arms against their sovereign. At this point the "Loyalists" withdrew from the revolutionary organization, leaving it in the hands of the more ardent spirits. These men, many of whom were new to positions of political leadership, were prepared to go all the way to defend their liberty.

While this pattern was developing, the royal governors and their associates did virtually nothing to interfere with the progress of events. Governor Franklin had no royal troops at his disposal, no police, no effective control over the militia. Moreover, the resistance movement commanded such general support down to the middle of 1775 that any drastic action on his part would have precipitated armed conflict. Thus, in New Jersey, the revolutionary cause was fully organized and in control of the state before it encountered any real efforts at suppression.

New Jersey embarked on statehood under auspices that were anything but promising. By August, 1776, Washington's patriot forces had suffered a series of disastrous reverses in New York, and it seemed merely a matter of weeks until New Jersey should be overrun. Internally, a civil war was going on. In some counties—especially Bergen, Monmouth, Essex, and Gloucester —Tory bands and rebel militia were engaged in vicious raids and skirmishes. Many of the experienced leaders of the state—in politics, law, religion, and business— had taken refuge with the British in New York. In the midst of all these trials a new and untested frame of government had to be put into operation.

The framers of the state constitution were exceedingly practical men, who recognized that they must eschew any novel or theoretical institutions of government and adhere as closely as possible to the colonial model. After all, no great political revolution had been demanded, only the curtailment of English interference. Consequently, almost the only alterations made in the government were those necessitated by the fact that there was no longer to be any connection with England: any corps of royally-appointed officials. Perhaps unwittingly, however, the sum effect of the changes was to produce a highly democratic government.

Power was strongly concentrated in the legislative branch of the government. There was a legislative council, made up of one member from each of the thirteen counties, and an assembly in which each county was initially to be represented by three members. Legislators were kept responsive to the will of their constituents by annual elections, held on the second Tuesday in October. Property qualifications similar to those that had prevailed under royal rule were continued. Councilmen had to be worth £1000 in real and personal property; the amount fixed for assemblymen was £500. Eligible to vote were all inhabitants of "full age" who had resided one year in the county and were worth £50.

Elections were conducted under very lax procedures. Typically, there was only one polling place in a county; in half of the counties voice voting persisted until several years after the Revolution; election officials were chosen by the assembled voters on the morning of the election and were usually strongly partial to one faction; the polling might continue for several days; and there were no effective safeguards against voting by ineligible persons. Nevertheless, it was possible for the vast majority of adult males to vote, and there is abundant evidence that the government reflected the wishes of the mass of the citizenry.

The General Assembly, as the two houses together were called, had almost unlimited legislative power. It could pass any laws except those which would abolish annual elections, trial by jury, or religious freedom. It was not even strictly bound by the constitution, except in those three particulars. In addition it was vested with significant appointive and judicial powers. All state officials and many on the county level were named by the two houses in joint meeting, including the governor, secretary of state, attorney-general, treasurer, supreme court justices, county judges, and justices of the peace. The council, sitting with the governor, constituted the highest court of appeals and also acted as a court of pardons. Obviously, the constitution was not based on the theory of separation of powers.

Mainly because of the long tradition of antagonism to the royal governors, the new constitution created an extremely weak chief executive. Chosen annually by the legislature, the governor had no veto, no power of appointment, no clearly stated executive functions. He presided over the council, held the title of captain general of the military forces, and—in his judicial capacity —served as chancellor and surrogate and presided over the court of appeals. Under William Livingston, who was governor from 1776 until his death in 1790, the office was actually not an insignificant one, but Livingston's strength derived more from his prestige, vigor, and ability than it did from the defined powers of his office.

The judicial organization was nearly identical with the colonial system. The only major changes were in the method of naming judges and in the fixing of definite terms of office for all judges. The new governor, as had his royal predecessors, filled the role of chancellor and surrogate. The council continued as the court of last resort, and the supreme court and the lower courts had the same jurisdiction as in the past.

The Constitution also contained a rudimentary bill of rights. Those accused of crimes were assured the same privileges of witnesses and counsel as their prosecutors. The estates of suicides were not forfeit, but were to descend to the heirs in the usual manner. All persons were guaranteed freedom of religion and were not to be compelled to attend or support any place of worship. No religious sect was to be established in the state in preference to another. All Protestant inhabitants were to enjoy full civil rights; non-Protestants were by implication placed in an inferior status. No judges or sheriffs or others holding positions of profit were eligible for election to the assembly. The right to trial by jury was held inviolable, as was the holding of annual elections. There was no provision made for amending the basic charter, an omission that was to cause some difficulties in the future.

That the Constitution was the product of highly uncertain times was evident in its final paragraph. Apparently at the instigation of Samuel Tucker—the President of the Provincial Congress and a man whose later actions raised doubts about his devotion to the patriot cause—it was provided that in the event of "a reconciliation between Great Britain and these Colonies" the Constitution should be "null and void." Curiously enough, the term "colony"—rather than "state"—was used throughout the document. But on July 17, 1776, the Congress resolved to "assume the style and title of the Convention of the State of New Jersey," and—in a technical sense—that date may be regarded as New Jersey's birthday.

The new frame of government was put into effect with

WILLIAM LIVINGSTON.
Nov 1783 – Ob 1790.

From the original painting in the possession of the Family.

Governor William Livingston

Elected the first governor of the state in 1776, Livingston served until his death in 1790. A devoted patriot, he gave unstinting support to the war effort and later was a respected member of the Constitutional Convention.

Courtesy of Princeton University

little difficulty. The General Assembly was scheduled to convene in Princeton for its first session on August 27, 1776, but not until three days later were there sufficient members in attendance to enable the two houses to organize. On Friday, August 30, a joint session was held in the Library Room of Nassau Hall to elect a governor. The vote resulted in a tie between William Livingston and Richard Stockton. The following morning, after some involved political maneuvering in which John Stevens played the key role, a second ballot was taken and Livingston was the victor.

The descendant of a prominent New York family, the State's first governor had retired to New Jersey in 1772 after a brilliant career as a lawyer and political leader in New York. There, in Elizabeth, he built "Liberty Hall" and looked forward to the quiet enjoyment of his farm, his library, and his many friends. Frequently a center of controversy, he was a vigorous writer on questions of public concern. He was not one of the earliest opponents of British measures, but in time he became an ardent republican and an unswervingly devoted patriot. Throughout the Revolution, despite the fact that his life was frequently in danger, he performed heroic services for the cause and earned the close friendship of General Washington. In the twilight of his career he represented the State in the Constitutional Convention of 1787. Year after year, until his death, the joint meeting re-elected him to the governorship, frequently with no opposition. He was, without doubt, the most respected political figure in the State and one of the nation's illustrious patriot leaders.

Divided Loyalties

The new State did not command the loyalty of all the people of New Jersey. Indeed, it may be questioned whether even a majority of citizens were affirmatively disposed toward independence. A large segment of the population, engaged in its own daily concerns and with only marginal interest in the raging controversy, was not inclined to make a decision either way. Others, averse to the break with the mother country, sought to remain passive or neutral. But thousands of sincere men and women, acting from a variety of motives, risked their lives and their fortunes to assert their loyalty to their sovereign.

It is not a simple matter to explain why some men chose the Tory side and others the Whig. There were men of wealth and position as well as humble men of small means in both camps. Probably basic factors of personality, not easy to define, were as influential in determining an individual's course of action as any economic or social considerations. With these reservations in mind, however, it is possible to describe certain groups as being predominantly in one camp or the other.

Strongly inclined toward Toryism were those who held important offices under the royal governor. Cortlandt Skinner, Attorney-general and speaker of the assembly, and his brother, Stephen, former East Jersey treasurer, both served actively on the British side. The Chief Justice, Frederick Smyth and his brother John; David Ogden, Supreme Court Justice; Isaac Ogden and John Antill, Sergeant and Secretary respectively of the Supreme Court, all became prominent Loyalists. Most of the members of the governor's council, including Peter Kemble, David Ogden, Frederick Smyth, James Parker, Stephen Skinner, Daniel Coxe, and John Lawrence were either open Loyalists or neutralists, as were the sheriffs of Burlington, Gloucester, Hunterdon, Middlesex, and Monmouth.

The East Jersey Board of Proprietors, made up of men with large landholdings, many of whom held high official posts, was largely Tory. The Anglican clergy, with only one exception, refused to give allegiance to the new State, and for much of the war period the churches were closed, except when they were in an area occupied by the British forces. Thomas Bradbury Chandler, rector of Elizabeth, went to England. Jonathan Odell, of Burlington, employed his satirical pen with taunting effectiveness against the rebels from his refuge in New York. In general, adherents of the Church of England were hostile to the Revolution.

The Quakers, essentially conservative and opposed to conflict, were in an awkward position. Most of them lamented the rupture between King and colony, and when the break came, they sought to remain apart from the struggle. Few became active patriots, and because of their pacifism many refused to contribute in any way to the war effort. The conservative branch of the Dutch Reformed Church—the Conferentie—was preponderantly Tory, especially in Bergen County.

A score of lawyers were Loyalists, as were some of the leading physicians, but only a small proportion of Tories came from the wealthy or socially prominent classes.

The hundreds of Jerseymen who served in the volunteer Loyalist regiments or in the hated Loyalists bands that engaged in marauding and plundering came from the farms and the workshops of the State. James Moody, plain Sussex farmer, together with 73 of his neighbors, went over to the British in 1777, apparently because he resented being badgered by rebel authorities. In Monmouth County, the common folk living around Shrewsbury were as violent in their attachment to the King as those near Freehold were to Washington.

Several hundred Tories suffered the confiscation of all their property, and with the end of the war they faced the dreary prospect of starting life anew in Canada, or in England, or elsewhere. Hundreds of others, who had yielded to expediency and had forsworn their allegiance to America when the British forces came into their area, later had to endure the taunts and attacks of their patriot neighbors. It was not at all unusual for brothers to be divided against brothers and fathers against sons. On the whole there was more bitterness displayed by the rebels toward their Tory countrymen than toward the British regulars.

The steadfast adherents to the Whig cause came from a variety of groups. Foremost, perhaps, were those of

New England or Scotch-Irish backgrounds and Presbyterian religious affiliations. From the one Presbyterian congregation in Elizabeth, for example, there were Governor Livingston; Abraham Clark, a signer of the Declaration of Independence; Elias Boudinot, who became president of the Continental Congress; General Matthias Ogden; General Elias Dayton; Captain Jonathan Dayton; and the zealous pastor, James Caldwell. At Princeton, the Reverend Doctor John Witherspoon preached Presbyterian doctrine and rebellion with equal vigor and success. In the hills of Morris and in the lower portions of Cumberland, where New England accents were strong, Whiggery was prevalent. The liberal, or Coetus, wing of the Dutch Reformed Church, especially in the Raritan Valley, furnished many patriot-leaders, among them Jacob R. Hardenbergh and Hendrick Fisher.

Several men of prominence cast their lot with the new regime. Among the members of the governor's council, Francis Hopkinson and Richard Stockton signed the Declaration of Independence; John Stevens entered the legislature and later presided over the State convention that ratified the Federal Constitution; and William Alexander became one of Washington's trusted generals in the Continental Army. Many able young lawyers rose rapidly to prominence in state affairs. Influential merchants as well as leading iron manufacturers served the cause of independence in various capacities.

There was no lack of skilled leadership on the Whig side, political, military, or civilian. But it is true that with the departure of many men who had formerly wielded great power an unusual opportunity existed for new men, many of them of little note before the war, to come into prominence. Such men, for example, as Abraham Clark, William Paterson, David Brearly, Elias Boudinot, and Andrew Sinnickson—all of relatively humble origins—attained high positions chiefly because of the revolutionary overturn of the old order.

For what ends were these men contending? In brief they were struggling to maintain the independence of

William Alexander, Lord Stirling

A major-general in the Continental Line and trusted confidante
of General Washington, William Alexander derived his claim
to a title from a lapsed Scottish earldom.

the new state and nation. More fundamental, they wanted to preserve their rights as they understood them. They were not at the outset seeking to make a revolution that would overthrow the foundations of colonial society or to bring about a radical shift of political power within New Jersey. Aside from independence they started out with no revolutionary ideas, no thoughts of radical innovations. In one sense, at least, they were conservatives; they wanted to conserve their ancient rights against British threats to curtail or destroy them.

In time, however, the ferment of those years gave rise to a new ideology, most eloquently expressed in the Declaration of Independence. Republican government, the equality of all men, the denial of inherited pre-eminence, the concept of a nation of united states—these were to be the revolutionary products of what had begun as a war for independence.

VII

FIGHTING FOR FREEDOM

Not without justification has New Jersey been called the "Cockpit of the Revolution." Because of its strategic location between New York and Philadelphia, it was to be the arena for contending armies throughout the war. During three winters it sheltered General Washington and the major portion of his Continental Army. On its soil were fought the important battles of Trenton, Princeton, Red Bank, Monmouth, and Springfield, as well as scores of minor engagements and skirmishes. No other state so generally and continuously felt the impact of the struggle for independence. The civil population, subjected to the exactions of both friends and foes, was constantly reminded that the State was a military frontier. State officials, harassed by internal strife and by sudden military emergencies, were placed under severe trials. For seven frightening years there was no peace for New Jersey.

Invasion and Retreat

New Jersey had more than a year after the opening clashes at Lexington and Concord to advance its military preparations. During that period it organized a militia system, with one or more regiments in each county. It had in addition raised three battalions for service in the Continental Army. On paper, at least, several thousand men were prepared to defend the new state and contribute to the national effort. But sad experience was to show that the militia—untrained, poorly led, badly supplied, and mustered for short periods—was rarely an effective force. They were employed during the early months of 1776 in guarding the eastern zone of the state and in suppressing Tory bands. The Continentals, later organized as a brigade under General William Maxwell, went off to participate in the ill-fated Canadian expedition and in the fighting against the Indians in New York State.

It was not until June, 1776, that New Jersey was made directly aware of her impending role in the conflict. Washington's army spent most of the first year of the war besieging the British forces in Boston. General William Howe, at last forced to evacuate that city in March, embarked for Halifax to await reinforcements. Early in July he arrived off New York with a great fleet of ships and an army that ultimately numbered thirty-four thousand men. Washington, meanwhile, with an effective force scarcely two-thirds that of the British, had moved down to attempt to defend the city. As Howe's forces ponderously mobilized to take the offensive, New Jersey was a scene of military bustle and confusion.

Washington detached General Hugh Mercer to organize a Flying Camp, composed of militia from Pennsylvania, Delaware, and Maryland, to guard against a British movement into New Jersey. From his headquarters at Perth Amboy, Mercer endured countless frustrations as he sought to organize his command. Militia companies came and went almost daily with the result that no orderly troop disposition could be made. The New Jersey Militia had been called into service, some of them to assist the main army in New York, others to man defense posts at home. But as the weeks dragged on without the anticipated attack, the men became restless and clamored to return to their homes. By the end of July most of them had been released.

A new militia plan was then developed under which men would serve alternate months, and in accordance with this extraordinary arrangement the citizen-soldiers began to return to duty in August. Inhabitants in the vicinity of the militia encampments complained bitterly about the deportment of the undisciplined troops, who were often compelled by circumstances to subsist on what they could gather from the countryside. Conscientious officers were driven to despair by the independent behavior of their men. Some, like William Livingston, who found himself a general in command of a militia troop near Elizabeth, were acutely aware of their lack of experience in dealing with the many new problems confronting them in their unfamiliar role. It was to be no simple task to mobilize resistance to the British invaders.

Late in August Howe launched his attack, and in the ensuing Battle of Long Island, Washington was forced to retreat. For the next two months, the American cause met with a series of reverses as Washington yielded New York City to the triumphant invaders and took refuge in Westchester. With the British sweeping all resistance before them the situation of New Jersey became increasingly critical. Mercer's ineffectual Flying Camp, reinforced by the New Jersey militia, was distributed along a wide front extending from Perth Amboy to Bergen County. At Paulus Hook, fortifications had been constructed to serve as part of the defenses of New York. Early in September work was begun on Fort Lee which was to be a companion-fort to Fort Washington on the other side of the Hudson. When New York fell, British ships moved into the upper harbor and Paulus Hook became untenable. On September 23 it had to be evacuated, and the British at once moved in, their first invasion of New Jersey territory.

Although Washington was successful in averting the destruction of his dwindling army, he was unable to start an offensive. Accepting the loss of New York, which remained under British control throughout the war, he prepared to halt a possible move by Howe toward Philadelphia by way of New Jersey. Early in November he sent Lord Stirling with eight regiments to occupy positions at Rahway and New Brunswick. Washington himself, with about five thousand men, crossed the Hudson to New Jersey and made a temporary camp at Hackensack in mid-November. His situation grew desperate when on November 16 Fort Washington was attacked and forced to surrender with twenty-five hundred men taken prisoners. This catastrophe placed Fort Lee in jeopardy. Washington gave orders to remove all stores and ammunitions from the doomed stronghold, but before these movements could be completed the British struck again. Lord Cornwallis, in a daring enterprise, crossed the Hudson and, guided by a local Tory, John Aldington, he ascended a little-used path up the Palisades at Closter Landing on November 20. As he moved rapidly toward Fort Lee, the surprised garrison, unable to attempt a defense, fled hurriedly to join the main forces at Hackensack, leaving great quantities of stores in the ill-fated fort.

At this moment the future appeared well-nigh barren of hope. New York had fallen, the army had been decimated by casualties and desertions, and confidence in Washington's leadership and in the American cause itself had been badly shaken. To many it seemed that one more vigorous offensive would crush the rebellion.

Washington, aware that his position at Hackensack was a weak one, put his discouraged army in motion toward Newark on November 21. There he issued a call for the New Jersey Militia to come to his assistance in order to ward off the anticipated invasion of the State by Howe. But the militia would not turn out, and Washington was obliged to move on to the Raritan at New Brunswick, where he again hoped to take up strong defensive positions. Again his plans had to be cast aside, for at that time the enlistment-terms of most of the Flying Camp troops expired, and his army was reduced to a mere four thousand weary men.

It was at this desperate moment that a familiar voice raised a cry that helped to rally the flagging spirits of the army and the nation. Tom Paine, whose pamphlet *Common Sense* had done so much to increase the sentiment for independence in 1776, served with the army during the depressing days of the retreat. Soldiering by day and writing in the chill evenings by the light of a campfire, with a drumhead as his desk, he penned the first lines of his *Crisis* essays at Newark:

> These are the times that try men's souls. The summer soldier and the sunshine patriot will, in this crisis, shrink from the service of his country; but he that stands it now, deserves the love and thanks of man and woman.

This stirring appeal, which was read to the troops on the eve of the battle of Trenton, gave eloquent form to the determination of those patriots who clung to the cause in its darkest hour.

A British army, meanwhile, was proceeding at a slow pace in pursuit of the harried Continentals. On the afternoon of December 1, two days after Washington had halted at New Brunswick, the advance guard of the royal forces reached the Raritan. Reluctantly, Washington was forced once more to resume his retreat across the State, and two days later he reached the Delaware at Trenton. The British, for reasons that have never been satisfactorily explained, delayed five days at the Raritan before resuming the chase.

In his retreat Washington had left a force of twelve hundred men at Princeton. After taking up all the boats along the Delaware, he moved back to Princeton on December 7 in the hope of stopping the British advance at that point. But the forces opposed to him were so much superior that he decided to withdraw his whole army across the Delaware. Scarcely had the last troops crossed the river when Howe and Cornwallis arrived at the east bank. Unable to find any boats, the British had to bring their pursuit to a halt. Because of their dilatory pursuit Washington had escaped once again, and the patriot army for the first time in weeks rested secure from attack. The retreat through New Jersey had ended.

TURNING THE TIDE

Although Washington's army had gained a respite from the weeks of British pressure, the future seemed anything but bright. There was still the possibility that Howe might attempt to push on to Philadelphia, the capital of the Confederation. The Continental Congress, fearful of such a move, had prudently adjourned to Baltimore. The Commander-in-Chief's first concern was to strengthen his shattered forces. Within a few days, he was joined by contingents of militia from Pennsylvania, Maryland, and New Jersey. He also called for reinforcements from General Charles Lee at North Castle and General Philip Schuyler at Albany. Lee, who had readily persuaded himself that Washington was incompetent to exercise command, procrastinated in a manner that was all but treasonable. He had reached Basking Ridge by December 13, when he was captured by a British patrol and taken to New York as a prisoner. General John Sullivan then took charge and joined Washington on December 20 with two thousand troops. On the same day five hundred men from Schuyler's forces arrived with Benedict Arnold. Now it was possible for Washington to consider a daring course of action.

The British commanders, Howe and Cornwallis, had concluded that the campaign had ended. They would wait until spring to complete the task of suppressing the rebellion. Accordingly, Howe went back to New York while Cornwallis put his forces into winter quarters. In an effort to occupy as much of the state as possible the redcoats and the German mercenaries were dispersed over a long front extending from the Hackensack to the Delaware. New Brunswick was the principal headquarters. Along the Delaware the Hessians occupied Burlington, Bordentown, and Trenton. At the last place Colonel Johann Rall, a seasoned officer, had fourteen hundred men. Despite his strength, he was nervous and uncomfortable because of the constant attacks made on his patrols by roving American forces. Due to his apprehension he was to commit a series of disastrous blunders.

While the military situation was changing its complexion, the civil population of New Jersey was in ferment. The legislature was forced to flee from Princeton to Trenton and then to Burlington, where it disbanded. For the time being only the Council of Safety, headed by the governor, sought to maintain some vestige of authority. As the British forces extended their occupation of the State, many who had been only lukewarm in their devotion to independence openly avowed their Loyalist sympathies. General Howe announced that all who would renew their allegiance to the Crown would be pardoned and guaranteed protection for their lives and property. Nearly three thousand men, including some members of the legislature, one signer of the Declaration of Independence, and a justice of the Supreme Court, accepted Howe's "protection."

Rebel leaders, fearing British vengeance, frantically sought to move their families to places of safety. Queen's College at New Brunswick and the College of New Jersey at Princeton, both centers of Whiggery, were temporarily disbanded when those towns became British strongholds. Some farmers became suddenly prosperous by selling their produce to British quartermasters. Others were ruined when marauding soldiers seized their crops, tore down their fences, and ransacked their dwellings. New Jersey had become virtually a no-man's-land.

Washington, whose courage and steadfastness had only been tested and strengthened by the months of adversity, decided that some bold action was necessary to inspire confidence in the patriot cause and to rally the dispirited people of New Jersey. He determined to attack Trenton. In a council of war on December 24 a plan was developed by which General John Cadwalader would cross the Delaware and engage the Hessians at Bordentown, General James Ewing would cross at Trenton and attempt to seize the bridge over the Assunpink, and the main body—under Washington—would cross at McKonkey's Ferry, above Trenton, and carry out the main offensive against Rall's garrison. This was a complicated plan involving many elements and with many variable factors. It might easily be upset by unfavorable conditions at the river crossings, by a breakdown in communications, or by faulty timing. Above all, there must be complete surprise.

The plan was put in motion on Christmas Day, 1776.

Cadwalader and Ewing set out for their objectives. Early in the evening the twenty-four hundred men under Washington began the hazardous crossing of the Delaware, which, choked with swiftly floating ice, tested the skill and endurance of the Marblehead fishermen under Colonel John Glover who were doing the ferrying. Utilizing large flat-bottomed Durham boats, which could carry fifty men with ease, the ragged army made the agonizing passage.

It was three o'clock in the morning—far behind schedule—when the troops were finally assembled for the advance. The army marched swiftly four miles inland to Birmingham (near today's Washington Crossing State Park) and then divided into two wings. One, under General John Sullivan, went to the right down the River Road. The other, under General Nathanael Greene, marched down the Pennington Road. Ahead of each lay a march of nearly ten miles over rutted, frozen roads through country where enemy patrols or Tory sympathizers might at any moment give the alarm that would doom the expedition to failure.

Marching with Washington on that desperate foray were heroic men who have become immortal in our history. In addition to Sullivan and Greene there were the brave Hugh Mercer, soon to perish at Princeton; Henry Knox, later chief of artillery and first United States Secretary of War; Arthur St. Clair, a Scottish veteran who commanded the Pennsylvania troops; the loyal Lord Stirling, a valiant figure despite his spendthrift habits and his pretensions to a lapsed Scottish earldom; and John Stark of New Hampshire, a veteran of Bunker Hill. Among the younger men were Alexander Hamilton and James Monroe, both of whom were to gain distinction in the ensuing encounter. Had their mission on that perilous night ended in failure, their names might now be unknown.

When the dawn arrived, the weary columns were still two miles from their destination. All hope of achieving surprise now seemed to be gone. But it was not until eight o'clock, when both wings of the army had reached the outskirts of Trenton, that the first contact was made with enemy outposts. Colonel Rall, despite obvious and repeated warnings, had failed to take the most elementary precautions, and his lightly-manned outposts were easily overwhelmed by the Americans. Within a matter of minutes both Sullivan and Greene had seized strategic locations for their artillery, and before the befuddled Rall could organize his men, the full attack was launched. Soon the little village was a scene of smoke-shrouded confusion as the disordered Hessians vainly sought to put up some semblance of defense. While attempting to rally his own shattered regiment, Rall fell from his horse mortally wounded. The leaderless remnants of his command were divided, surrounded, and compelled to surrender. The entire engagement had lasted only an hour and a half.

As Washington surveyed the ravaged town, he must have indulged himself in a feeling of triumph. The American casualties amounted to only four men wounded, one of whom was Lieutenant James Monroe. Three Hessian regiments had been destroyed, with over a hundred killed or wounded and nine hundred taken prisoners. Some four hundred had managed to escape and join Colonel Karl Emil von Donop. The attack had succeeded beyond all expectation, despite the fact that Cadwalader and Ewing had found it impossible to get across the river to carry out their missions.

Soon after the battle Washington and his commanders held a council of war to decide on the next move. The men were near exhaustion; there was the danger of a counterattack from Princeton or Bordentown; and the large number of prisoners had to be securely guarded. Reluctantly, they decided to return to the Pennsylvania encampment at once. It was after dark when the last of the men, most of whom had been marching and fighting for thirty-six hours and had traveled nearly forty miles in miserable weather, reached their sodden tents. They had won a spectacular victory, one that turned the long-running tide of defeat.

The British were thrown into confusion by Washington's surprise maneuver. They had committed the error of dispersing their forces too widely, and they had paid the penalty. Now they hurriedly set about consolidating their detachments. Colonel von Donop and his Hessians, who had left Bordentown and Burlington at the first word of Washington's victory, joined General Alexander Leslie's regiments at Princeton. The garrison at New Brunswick under General James Grant was also reinforced. Meanwhile, several American detachments, emboldened by recent successes, augmented the alarm of the royal forces by conducting annoying raids on supply trains and isolated outposts. Overnight the initiative had passed to the Americans.

Washington was fully alert to the new opportunities that presented themselves. After resting his troops, he recrossed the Delaware and by December 30 was again in Trenton. There he was soon joined by Cadwalader's men, who had managed to cross the river on December 27, and by a smaller body under General Thomas Mifflin. His total force numbered a little over five thousand. There was a brief crisis when the enlistments of a considerable body of the soldiers expired with the end of the year, but most of them were induced to remain in service when Washington pledged his personal credit to assure them a bounty. With his battle-tested army mobilized, the commander considered his next move. The week's delay had enabled the British to reorganize. By January 2, eight thousand men under General Cornwallis were on the march from Princeton toward Trenton. Aware that his position was not defensively strong, but loath to dash the spirit of his men by another retreat, Washington decided to dig in and meet the enemy.

Advance parties were sent out to slow Cornwallis' march, and they operated to such good effect that he did not reach Trenton until dusk. After a brief skirmish at long range, the British commander decided to wait for daylight before launching his main effort. Late that night Washington took counsel with his generals. He hesitated to risk an engagement with Cornwallis because of the unfavorable terrain. Someone, possibly Colonel Joseph Reed, proposed that the patriot army attempt to circle the enemy's left flank that night and move by way of Sandtown (now Mercerville) and the new Quaker Bridge Road to Princeton. There they might strike a blow at Colonel Charles Mawhood's brigade and then attempt to capture the lightly guarded British military chest of funds at New Brunswick.

At one o'clock in the morning of January 3, while fires were kept burning along the American front to deceive the enemy, the brilliant maneuver was started. By dawn the army was within two miles of Princeton near the Stony Brook Meeting House. While Washington and the main body continued across Thomas Clark's farm toward the center of Princeton, a small force under General Mercer marched toward the Princeton-Trenton road to destroy the bridge over Stony Brook and thereby slow the anticipated pursuit by Cornwallis. He was within sight of his objective when he was suddenly attacked and routed by a superior force under Colonel Mawhood. Colonel Cadwalader's Pennsylvanians attempted to aid Mercer, but they too were thrown back in confusion. Then Washington appeared on the scene, rallied his troops for the attack, and soon the remnants of enemy regiments were fleeing toward Trenton. A second skirmish took place with two other British regiments closer to Princeton, but again the resistance was short lived. The British losses were heavy: one hundred dead and three hundred prisoners. The Americans suffered about forty casualties, among them the irreplaceable General Mercer, who died nine days later from his wounds.

Meanwhile, Cornwallis had at last discovered the ruse that had been perpetrated on him and was driving his troops up the road from Trenton to Princeton. On the way he was met by the fleeing survivors of Mawhood's command, who told him the bitter news of Washington's victory. Pressing on with all speed, the British advance guard reached Princeton by noon to discover that Washington had moved on. Although the British had abandoned their pursuit at this point, Washington and his generals gave up the idea of continuing on to New

Brunswick. The men had been marching and fighting almost steadily since the previous day, and no one was certain of the disposition of the British forces. Above Kingston the army turned to the left and, following the route of the Millstone River, tramped through the cold night until it reached the tiny hamlet of Millstone. Having covered thirty miles in the preceding twenty-four hours, the exhausted but victory-stirred men huddled together around their campfires for such rest as they could manage throughout the wintry night. The next day they resumed their march northward until they reached Morristown, where on January 7 they entered upon their long winter encampment.

Within the brief span of two weeks, Washington had by his great daring and resourcefulness entirely altered the military balance in New Jersey. When he took up his position in the hills of Morristown, the British were obliged to concentrate their forces in the small region between New Brunswick and Perth Amboy. By January 10 there were fourteen thousand British, Hessian, and Anspach troops crowded into these garrison towns, where they spent an exceedingly uncomfortable winter virtually in a state of siege. Most of the state, free of the occupying invaders, was returned to Whig control. Perhaps more important, the whole patriot cause had been rescued from the dangers of despondency. Cornwallis and Howe had lost the best opportunity they would ever have to bring the war to an end. Trenton and Princeton marked the turning point of the war.

THE INTERMINABLE WAR

Despite the apparently favorable complexion of military affairs, Washington faced grave problems during the winter months at Morristown. The terms of enlistment of his Continental troops—raised as the "First Establishment"—had expired, and by February there were fewer than four thousand in camp, most of them short-term militia from Pennsylvania. Congress, meanwhile, devised ambitious plans for raising an army of seventy-five thousand but the states responded slowly and inadequately to the calls made upon them, with the result that the Commander-in-Chief scarcely knew what sort of army he would be able to place in the field. He hoped to free himself from reliance on the militia—"this mixed, motley, crew," he called them—but in this he was to be disappointed. In the spring new regiments began to arrive from Virginia, Maryland, Delaware, Pennsylvania, and New Jersey, until by May Washington had nine thousand men.

During this first winter encampment at Morristown, the army endured the privations that were to be experienced later at Valley Forge, Middlebrook, and at the second Morristown camp. The troops were housed in rude huts in the Loantaka Valley, southeast of the village, while Washington had his headquarters at Arnold's Tavern. Because of the incredibly inefficient supply organization, there were chronic shortages of food and clothing, making it necessary at times for Washington to commandeer sustenance for his men from the local farmers. Disease took a heavy toll, although a mass inoculation of the troops for smallpox in February effectively curbed that dreaded scourge. Whether from boredom or necessity, marauding soldiers made themselves obnoxious to the local inhabitants by their depredations. The arrival of Martha Washington in mid-March relieved the tedium of camp routine, but the wrangling of officers over rank and precedence, constant anxiety about the slow progress of recruiting, and concern that the British might launch an offensive while his forces were still weak permitted Washington little occasion for relaxation.

Although there were no major military developments during the winter, there were frequent raids on British outposts and skirmishes between scouting parties. The area between New Brunswick and Bound Brook, where General John Lincoln commanded an advance party, was the scene of numerous clashes, as the Continentals sought to keep the British penned in their garrisons. On April 14 Cornwallis led a force of four thousand men in a surprise raid on Bound Brook, forcing Lincoln into a precipitous retreat, but by the time that General Greene arrived from Basking Ridge with reinforcements, the British had retired to New Brunswick.

Uncertain whether Howe planned an overland march against Philadelphia or a dash northward to the Hudson valley, Washington at the end of May moved his army down to Middlebrook, a strong position in the Watchung Mountains above Bound Brook. Two weeks later Howe began a series of maneuvers that puzzled Washington and tested his skill as a tactician. Moving out of Perth Amboy and New Brunswick, the British took up positions between Middlebush and Millstone on June 14 and began to construct redoubts, apparently hoping to lure the Continentals into a major engagement. Washington prudently avoided the trap, and five days later Howe withdrew to New Brunswick. On June 21 the British were again in motion, this time toward Perth Amboy. Washington cautiously ordered his army forward on June 24, sending Lord Stirling to Metuchen and establishing his own headquarters at Quibbletown (New Market) . Two days later the British moved quickly out of Perth Amboy, drove Stirling back to Westfield, and induced Washington to return to Middlebrook. But, again, the foray was not followed up. The British returned to Perth Amboy and from there, on July 1, crossed over to Staten Island.

Thus the New Jersey campaign, which had begun so auspiciously for the invaders on November 20, 1776, came to an inglorious end. After months of effort, the British retained only Paulus Hook, which remained under their control until the end of the war. The tide had been turned by the victories at Trenton and Princeton; and Washington, by confining the enemy to the small area of the lower Raritan valley and maintaining his own army intact, was able to retain the advantage, prevent an overland attack on Philadelphia, and force the British withdrawal from the State. Never again was New Jersey to suffer so disastrously from invasion, although throughout the remainder of the war it was to be a battleground and a highway for the contending armies.

After weeks of uncertainty regarding the destination of Howe's fleet-borne army, Washington concluded late in August that Philadelphia was the objective and prepared to defend the capital of the Confederation. Despite his efforts at Brandywine and Germantown, the British entered Philadelphia on September 25, and for the next two months attention focused on the Delaware, which was defended above Chester by forts and obstructions. Howe had to clear the river in order to supply his army. The two keys to the defense of the Delaware were Fort Mercer, at Red Bank, below Gloucester, on the New Jersey shore, and Fort Mifflin, on Mud Island across the river. On October 24, a force of two thousand Hessians under Count von Donop sought to take Fort Mercer, but they were repulsed by the small garrison with heavy losses, including their gallant commander. After Fort Mifflin fell to heavy bombardment in mid-November, Fort Mercer had to be evacuated when Cornwallis approached it with an overwhelming force.

In December Washington went into camp at Valley Forge, but throughout the winter New Jersey was harassed by constant raids. The southern counties were plundered by foraging parties from both armies and were kept in turmoil by the activities of the Loyalist West Jersey Volunteers. Meanwhile, the patriot-authorities were powerless to prevent extensive illegal trading with the enemy, both in New York and Philadelphia, and in certain counties—notably Bergen and Monmouth—a savage guerrilla warfare was carried on between Whig and Tory neighbors.

The summer campaign opened on June 17, 1778, when the British army, now led by Sir Henry Clinton, crossed the Delaware and began a hazardous march through New Jersey. Washington crossed the river near Lambertville, sent the youthful Lafayette ahead to harass the enemy, and sought a favorable opportunity to strike a major blow. The two armies were nearly equal in size. Clinton was encumbered by an enormous supply train, and Washington's troops had profited from the training they had received under General Frederick von Steuben's tutelage at Valley Forge.

Learning that Clinton had halted his march near Monmouth Court House (Freehold), Washington directed General Charles Lee to engage the enemy while he prepared to bring forward the main body of the army. The American attack was launched at ten o'clock in the morning on Sunday, June 28, and initially the advantage was with the Continentals. But when British reinforcements were thrown into action, some of Lee's troops were forced to draw back. At this point Lee, who seems to have lacked enthusiasm for the plan of battle, ordered a general withdrawal, and considerable disorder ensued.

Washington met the retreating troops, headed by their discredited commander, and after an angry exchange in which Washington's temper flared and Lee responded with characteristic insolence, Washington assumed command and desperately sought to reorganize his troops. Hour after hour the battle raged across the fields and ravines near Old Tennent Church. With the temperature soaring to nearly one hundred degrees, men and horses died from sheer exhaustion. By nightfall, after the longest continuous engagement of the Revolution, the American front had been re-established. Late that evening Clinton withdrew his battered regiments and resumed his march to Sandy Hook. Washington concluded that his men were too fatigued to continue the pursuit. The battle was indecisive, but it had demonstrated that American troops were sufficiently disciplined to meet British and Hessian regulars on equal terms in the open field.

After Monmouth the weary army marched northward to the Raritan, where in the open fields at Raritan Landing, opposite New Brunswick, the men were permitted a few days of rest. The highlight of this bivouac was the observance of the second anniversary of American independence, which was celebrated by a grand review. The troops, their hats festively adorned with green sprigs, lined the New Brunswick bank of the Raritan, and after General Washington and his aides had ridden past, thirteen cannon saluted the memorable day and the men fired three rounds of their muskets. Then the army, refreshed and with renewed dedication to the cause, set off for New York to spend the summer keeping Clinton's forces under close surveillance.

The approach of winter brought Washington back to New Jersey. Late in November troops began to arrive at Middlebrook, where they set to work constructing orderly rows of huts in the vicinity of the gap at Chimney Rock and some miles away near the hamlet of Weston. The artillery park, under General Henry Knox, was based at Pluckemin. Washington established his headquarters in the Wallace House, on the outskirts of Somerville. In contrast to Valley Forge, the encampment was relatively comfortable because of the mildness of the winter, improvements in the supply arrangements, and the remoteness of the enemy. Mrs. Washington, as was her custom, joined her husband in the spring, and a remarkably gay social season, enlivened by visits from foreign dignitaries, ensued. In June, 1779, the veteran army again set off for New York, taking with them pleasant memories of their months in the Somerset hills.

At the close of the uneventful summer campaign, Washington again selected Morristown as the site for his winter encampment. There he could keep a watchful eye on the British in New York City and be in a position to move by well guarded routes either to the Hudson or the Delaware. There, too, he could maintain secure contact with the states to the south, from which he drew men and supplies. Furthermore, the hilly country around Morristown made his position secure from attack. The several divisions of his army constructed their villages of huts in Jockey Hollow, three miles southwest of the town, while Washington and his official family occupied the Ford house on the outskirts of Morristown.

The winter was the most severe since 1755. When the main body of troops arrived in December the snow was already two feet deep, and by January a succession of storms had piled drifts six and seven feet high. So intense and prolonged was the cold that the swiftest streams froze, making it impossible for the local mills to grind grain for the starving army. The Arthur Kill, between New Jersey and Staten Island, was solidly frozen, which inspired General Stirling to attempt a sleigh-borne attack in January on Loyalist regiments based there. But the islanders had been warned of the raid, repulsed it with ease, and retaliated by burning the Presbyterian church in Elizabeth and the academy in Newark. Not even at Valley Forge had the soldiers experienced such cruel privations, but they were now hardened veterans, with implicit confidence in their heroic commander, and they somehow survived trials that seemed beyond human endurance.

As the war entered its sixth year, the prospect of ultimate victory still seemed distant. For four years New Jersey had been a principal theater of war. It had sheltered Washington's army through three winters and had been ravaged as no other state had been. From the Hackensack to the Rancocas, every town bore the scars of the long conflict. Weariness with the war and unredressed grievances produced ugly mutinies among the regular troops and apathy and shirking on the part of the militia. In June, months of discouragement were climaxed by the bitter news that Clinton had taken Charleston, capturing General Lincoln and his Southern Army, and was heading back to New York, presumably to reassume the offensive in that area.

The intentions of the British, seemingly, were forecast by a sudden raid from Staten Island by a large force under General Wilhelm von Knyphausen on the night of June 6, 1780. Colonel Elias Dayton's regiment of the New Jersey Brigade, aided by hastily assembled militia, fell back from Elizabeth before the superior strength of the enemy through Connecticut Farms (Union) to the outskirts of Springfield. Meanwhile Washington hurried down from Morristown to Short Hills, anticipating a major offensive. But after burning Connecticut Farms, and wantonly killing the wife of the Reverend James

Ford Mansion, Morristown

Headquarters of General Washington and his aides during the winter encampment of 1779-1780. Mrs. Washington spent part of the winter with her husband, as was her custom.

Courtesy of National Park Service, Morristown

Caldwell, the invaders withdrew to Elizabeth Town Point. After waiting for several days for the British to disclose the object of their campaign, Washington proceeded to Pompton with the main body of his army, leaving General Greene with a corps at Springfield. On June 23 von Knyphausen struck again, this time with two powerful columns that joined near Springfield and succeeded in forcing Greene out of the village. After achieving this success, however, the invaders, tormented by pursuing militia, retreated, this time to the safety of Staten Island. The motives of these two Knyphausen raids puzzled contemporary observers as much as they have later historians. Whatever their purpose, they were the last major invasions in force that New Jersey was to experience.

The movements of Washington and his Continentals back and forth across the State form the main theme of the story of the Revolution in New Jersey, but many other incidents of heroism and villainy would have to be recalled if the narrative of those hectic years was to be complete. Scarcely a month passed when British regulars, Loyalists, or guerrilla bands of "Refugees" were not bringing bloodshed and destruction to some portion of the state.

Typical of this side of the war was the foray conducted by the dreaded Simcoe Raiders through the Raritan Valley in October, 1779, which left in its train smoldering houses, ruined crops, and lasting hatreds. In Monmouth, David Forman's "Retaliators," a Whig protective association, carried on what amounted to a reign of terror only slightly less outrageous than the plundering expeditions of the infamous Tory gang headed by John Bacon.

Along the coast, from New Brunswick to Mays Landing, scores of privateers preyed with extraordinary success on British shipping and provoked retaliatory attacks. One of the major centers of this legalized freebooting was Chestnut Neck, on the Little Egg Harbor, which was shelled and burned in October, 1779. A similar assault on Toms River in 1782 produced international repercussions when, in reprisal for the murder of the local commander, Captain Joshua Huddy, a young British captive, Captain Charles Asgill, was selected by lot to pay with his life for a deed in which he had had no part. The intervention of the highest authorities in England and France ultimately induced Washington to free the innocent hostage.

Throughout the war deeds of heroism were matched by sordid and wicked transactions at the expense of the cause. Prominent patriots were not above buying salt at Toms River for fifteen dollars a bushel and selling it to the troops at Morristown for thirty-five dollars. The Quartermaster General and his two deputies sought to profit from their investment in the Batsto iron works, from which they made large purchases in their official capacities. Farmers engaged as a matter of course in selling their produce to the British in New York. So widespread was this evil that Washington confessed in exasperation that even if he were to assign to his entire army the task of preventing the traffic, it would still continue.

While many were becoming wealthy by speculating and profiteering, those who bore the brunt of the war and endured the terrors and privations of campaigns and camps—the Continental soldiers—habitually found their miserable pay months in arrears. Reduced to desperation by their tragic plight, the Pennsylvania troops stationed at Morristown under General Wayne mutinied on New Year's Day, 1780, and set off for Philadelphia to demand redress of their grievances. Later in the same year the New Jersey Brigade engaged in a similar protest at Pompton.

Toryism was a persistent problem throughout the war. No accurate estimate can be made of the numbers of those who adhered to the British cause, but there is basis for the belief that New Jersey had as high a proportion of active Loyalists as any other state. Cortlandt Skinner, former assembly speaker and attorney-general of the colony, recruited six battalions of Loyalists from the State by 1778. The properties of hundreds of Loyalists were confiscated and sold under legislation enacted in 1777, and when the war ended thousands of erstwhile Jerseymen went into a harsh exile in Nova Scotia rather than endure the taunts of their old neighbors.

Larger numbers of Tories, while not taking an active part in the conflict, covertly opposed the Whig cause. In Bergen County, as late as 1782, the patriot-party found it impossible to prevent the election of known Tories to the legislature, and in Burlington, where the Tories and Quakers often made common political cause, the Whigs were able to retain control only by using the militia to dominate the polls. "I have seen tories members of Congress," deplored Governor Livingston, "judges upon tribunals, tories representatives in our Legislative councils, tories members of our Assemblies . . ." In many respects the bitterest side of the struggle was this fratricidal conflict that divided neighbors, churches, and even families.

BETWEEN WAR AND PEACE

New Jersey witnessed what was to be the march toward final victory in the seemingly interminable war late in August, 1781. Crossing the Hudson three days apart and moving by separate routes until they converged at Princeton, the French and American armies under the Comte de Rochambeau and Washington hastened southward to Yorktown. There, with the invaluable aid of the French fleet, they secured a decisive victory that brought about the surrender of Cornwallis and his army. When the glorious news reached New Jersey late in October, there was widespread rejoicing, and in mid-December the State observed a general day of thanksgiving. There was a common feeling that peace would soon be restored, but a year and a half passed before word was received that a preliminary treaty had been signed January 20, 1783. Then, on April 19, came the official proclamation suspending all further hostilities. Many more months were to go by before the definitive treaty was signed on September 3, but in the meantime the difficult transition from war to peace was begun.

As soon as hostilities ended there was a considerable movement of people across the lines that had so long separated the adversaries. Businessmen rushed to New York City to collect debts from Tory creditors about to depart for England or Nova Scotia. Fathers and sons, brothers and sisters, supporters of opposing causes, were reunited after years of anguish. British and Hessian officers welcomed the opportunity to become tourists, and many were attracted to the natural wonders of the Passaic Falls. Continental troops, still unpaid, returned home on furlough while awaiting their final discharge.

The imminence of peace also enabled people to take stock of the terrible losses they had suffered. Scarcely a church or school building in any of the towns from Hackensack to Trenton had not been destroyed or seriously damaged. Wherever the armies had marched or camped, they had left scars on the landscape. In Middlesex County alone the properties of 655 individuals had been damaged extensively by British or American troops, and the toll in Bergen was probably greater.

But the damage and disruption went beyond the physical havoc. Trade, and the economy in general, had been thoroughly disorganized. Churches, especially those like the Anglican, the Dutch Reformed, and the Lutheran that had strong connections abroad, faced profound readjustments. Educational institutions had all but gone out of existence, libraries had been plundered, and many of the most cultivated men in the state had fled into exile. The very fabric of society had been torn by the clash between Whigs and Tories, and its economic base had been altered by the confiscation and sale of the properties of the Loyalists.

Not the least cost was that represented by the expenditure of military energies. Although precise figures are not obtainable, there were probably some four thousand men who had served in the New Jersey Brigade or other units of the Continental Army. An additional ten thousand probably saw duty with the State troops, the militia, or as wagonmasters, commissaries, or guides. The Jersey Continentals had left their dead and wounded on the fields of Quebec, the Brandywine, Germantown, Monmouth, and Yorktown, and the militia had been called upon in innumerable emergencies within the State. Civilians and soldiers alike had paid a heavy price, some zealously and others with reluctance, for the cause of independence.

The final scene of this memorable era that witnessed the birth of a new nation occurred, appropriately enough, in the State where defeat had first been transformed into victory. The Continental Congress, driven from Philadelphia by the threats of mutinous Pennsylvania troops, moved to Princeton late in June, 1783, and made that small but delightful town the capital of the new nation until their adjournment early in November. Congress held its sessions in the newly-repaired Library Room of Nassau Hall. President of the Continental Congress Elias Boudinot, one of New Jersey's most distinguished statesmen, established himself at Morven, the residence of his sister, where he entertained on a lavish scale.

The highlight of the session was provided by General Washington's ten-weeks visit for the purpose of consulting with Congress on the final arrangements for the demobilization of his army. It was at his temporary residence in the Berrien house at Rocky Hill that he entertained the members of Congress at a dinner made memorable by his relaxed, even witty, mood; and it was there that he drafted his "Farewell Orders to the Armies of the United States."

Bidding his troops "an affectionate, a long farewell," the Commander-in-Chief recalled how a disciplined army had been formed from raw materials, how men drawn from every part of the Union had become "but one patriotic band of Brothers." Expressing confidence that those who had sacrificed so much in the cause of freedom would prove themselves "not less virtuous and useful as Citizens, than they have been persevering and victorious

Elias Boudinot

An early participant in the Revolutionary movement, Boudinot was president of the Continental Congress in 1783. He later served in the Federal Congress and as director of the United States mint.

Courtesy of Princeton University

as Soldiers," he offered in their behalf a prayer to the "God of Armies":

May ample justice be done them here, and may the choicest of heaven's favours, both here and hereafter, attend those who, under the devine auspices, have secured innumerable blessings for others; with these wishes, and this benediction, the Commander in Chief is about to retire from Service. The Curtain of separation will soon be drawn, and the military scene to him will be closed for ever.

At last, on November 1, the glorious news was received that the definitive Treaty of Peace had been signed in Paris. Princeton, New Jersey, and the entire Nation rejoiced and gave thanks that the war for independence had been won and that the United States had taken their rightful place among the nations of the world.

VIII

EXPERIMENT IN INDEPENDENCE

As the war came to an end, New Jersey, in company with her sister states, faced formidable problems. A new nation, made up of loosely confederated states governed in accordance with republican principles, had come into being, but it remained to be determined whether these novel political experiments would succeed. The times themselves presented special difficulties. The long war had disorganized the economy of the State, disrupted its society, brought ruin to its farms and buildings, and produced a staggering burden of debt. With the return of peace, the people of the State, operating through their untested political institutions and with scant assistance from the central government, set about the manifold tasks of readjustment and reconstruction. Their success in meeting the challenges that confronted them was remarkable. By 1787 the State had dealt satisfactorily with its own problems and then participated enthusiastically in the formation of a new Federal Union in order that the benefits of independence and republicanism might be enjoyed to the fullest.

Readjustment and Reconstruction

The frame of government that had been devised so hastily for the new state in 1776 had survived the trials of the war years unaltered. Because it placed virtually all authority in the hands of an annually elected legislature, which was unchecked either by the veto power of the governor or by the central government, it was ex-

tremely democratic. Under the liberal and loosely en-
forced suffrage provisions, all but a small fraction
of white males could vote, and elections were frequently
tumultuous affairs that drew to the polls most of the
eligible electorate. Two significant changes had been
made in the election machinery during the war years.
The ballot replaced the voice-vote in several counties,
and the number of polling places was greatly increased.
This latter development was particularly important, for
it made the polls easily accessible to the voters, and thus
had the effect of stimulating participation.

Although there was a lively interest in politics,
political parties, in the sense that we use the term today,
had not yet appeared. Within individual counties rival
factions contended for office. In Burlington, for example,
there were severe contests at the polls between Whig and
Tory factions down through 1784, and in other counties
there was rivalry between sections or personalities, but
the alignments were not stable and varied from county
to county.

Within the legislature, there was commonly a cleavage
between the members from East Jersey and those from
West Jersey. In addition to traditional antagonisms, this
split reflected disagreements over certain of the leading
issues of the period. One source of controversy was the
effort of the West Jersey proprietors to enlist the aid of
the legislature in drawing a new boundary line between
the two divisions that would have added substantially
to their holdings. The Eastern proprietors balked this
move by soliciting the support of members from their
region. Even more serious was conflict over financial
questions, which usually found the West Jersey representatives united in opposition to the "soft money"
policies of their East Jersey adversaries. Whatever their
differences, the legislators proved to be highly responsive
to the vigorously expressed will of their constituents and
alert to the tides of opinion within the State.

Political leadership underwent some significant
changes during the postwar years. With the return of
peace many of the foremost public figures resigned their

offices to resume their business and professional careers. Elias Boudinot, a prominent member of the Continental Congress; William Paterson, wartime attorney-general; Robert Morris, the first chief justice of the State; and many others, returned to private pursuits. These departures doubtless weakened the government. On the other hand, Governor William Livingston, who had performed such heroic services during the war, remained at his post until his death in 1790, and by the force of his personality and his frequent newspaper essays exerted a strong influence on public affairs. The other pre-eminent figure of the period was Livingston's fellow-townsman, Abraham Clark, a man of humble origins and strong democratic principles. A signer of the Declaration of Independence, Clark left the Continental Congress after the war to serve in the State legislature, where he became the leader of the East Jersey delegations and a spirited champion of popular causes.

The State's political order had survived the war relatively unscathed, but its cultural and religious institutions had been seriously impaired. Contemporary observers in 1783 were appalled at the many evidences of moral and religious laxity, ignorance, and viciousness. But within a few years of determined effort much of the ground that had been lost was regained. The State's two colleges, Rutgers and Princeton, made rapid recoveries. Rutgers resumed operations in New Brunswick in 1781, after having led a precarious existence at Millstone and North Branch since 1776. Princeton never suspended operations and graduated a record class in 1786. The older academies were soon flourishing and new ones were established at Trenton, Bordentown, and elsewhere. The State medical society was revived in 1781 and other societies for promoting "useful knowledge" were formed. There had been only one newspaper in the state in 1777—the *New Jersey Gazette*—but by 1787 there were four.

The churches of New Jersey, many of which had lost their buildings and their ministers, faced a desperate challenge. Half of the Presbyterian congregations were without regular pastors, and at the war's end there were only three Anglican clergymen to serve members of that denomination. By dint of considerable sacrifice, and some assistance from state-authorized lotteries, church buildings were slowly rehabilitated and, in due course, new clergymen were trained. At the same time the Presbyterians, Dutch Reformed, and Anglican (now Episcopalian) churches adopted new forms of national organization to conform to the conditions created by independence.

In a related field, the Revolution had stimulated humanitarian concerns and produced important reforms. The ideology of the Declaration of Independence was at least partially responsible for modifications in the institution of slavery. In 1786 the legislature forbade the further importation of slaves, and two years later masters were prohibited from removing slaves from the State without their consent and were required to teach their slaves how to read. The Quakers sought to bring about the abolition of slavery, but not until 1804, when provision was made for gradual emancipation, was any progress made in this direction. The new spirit of the times was also reflected in laws ending the aristocratic practices of entail and primogeniture.

The rehabilitation of the war-ravaged economy was the most difficult challenge of all and the one which most absorbed the interest of the State's lawmakers. During the two final years of the war, boom conditions prevailed. Extensive illegal trading with the British in New York City brought considerable quantities of hard money, as well as imported goods to stock the country stores, into the State. But by 1784 the boom had collapsed, British merchants restricted credit, and little specie remained in circulation. For the next few years there were widespread complaints of currency shortages, burdensome taxes, and economic stagnation.

The farmers of the State, in part because of their poor agricultural practices, were hard pressed to meet their private debts and pay their taxes. To add to their difficulties, the wheat crop was devastated after 1786 by the ravages of the Hessian fly. The large landholders, as represented by the East Jersey proprietors, were in dire straits. The Board of Proprietors was unable to meet during the war because all its records, and many of its members, were in New York City. In the interim the lands of the absentee proprietors had been pillaged, tenants had refused to pay the customary rents, and many estates had been confiscated, broken up, and sold. The iron industry, which had prospered as a result of wartime demands, experienced a severe depression, although normal production was resumed by 1789.

Merchants welcomed the return of peace with high anticipations. They had long resented the State's commercial subservience to New York and Philadelphia, and they hoped that the altered political situation would make it possible for them to develop an independent trade with Europe. Accordingly they applauded the decision of the legislature in 1783 not to impose any tariffs on imports. Because both New York and Pennsylvania had tariffs on goods from abroad, New Jersey traders expected that their ports would enjoy special advantages. New York was sufficiently irritated by New Jersey's free-trade policy to enact measures designed to prevent the smuggling of tariff-free goods across the Hudson. In retaliation, New Jersey imposed an annual tax of £30 on the lighthouse that New York had erected on Sandy Hook. The merchants also devised an elaborate proposal to make Perth Amboy and Burlington "free ports," endowed with privileges that might attract traders to concentrate there, but the legislature did not fully implement the plan. By 1787 the efforts to enter into competition with the neighboring cities had ended, and trade had resumed its customary prewar pattern. New Jersey merchants lacked the capital resources to engage in extensive foreign commerce, and they contented themselves with the modest, but safe, returns to be derived from shipping locally.

While individuals sought to work out their own economic destinies, the legislature wrestled with incredibly complex problems of currency, debts, and taxes. It had somehow to levy and collect taxes to meet enormous debts accumulated during the war and at the same time create a currency system without any specie to sustain it. In accomplishing these objectives it displayed amazing ingenuity.

Late in the war the State had issued $291,000 in paper currency to replace $7,000,000 in depreciated Continental currency. This "new emission" money, as it was called, was to be withdrawn from circulation by taxes over a period of six years, but in the meantime it depreciated until by 1784 it was worth only one-third of its face value. As the currency was contracted, debtors found it increasingly difficult to meet their obligations and demanded the issuance of more paper money. By 1786, when the currency in circulation was less than two dollars a person and when State taxes equaled two-thirds of the total money supply, the distress was acute. Several thousand citizens flooded the legislature with petitions demanding the enactment of a loan-office measure on the familiar colonial model.

Whereas in the colonial period all segments of society had welcomed this particular type of paper currency, now there were strong objections from conservative, creditor groups. They had seen how during and after the war legislatures had issued paper money but subsequently had repudiated their promise to redeem it, and they held justifiable fears that the loan-office money would meet a like fate. But after a severe struggle lasting over several months and producing heated debates in the newspapers and in the legislature, the desired act was passed.

The measure called for the issuance of £100,000 to be lent on landed security for a period of twelve years at six per cent interest. The money was to be full legal tender, and the interest received annually was to be used for the support of the government. Contrary to the fears of the conservatives, the money held its value well and met the desperate need for an adequate currency. The plight of debtors was further ameliorated by several laws liberalizing bankruptcy procedures, permitting debts to be paid in public securities, and simplifying court actions.

Although the legislature pursued "soft money" policies and was responsive to the demands of debtors, it sought at the same time to keep faith with the public creditors. New Jersey's citizens held a disproportionately large share of Continental securities of various types, amounting in all to perhaps two million five hundred thousand dollars. Half of this sum was represented by Continental Loan Office Certificates (comparable to War Bonds) and the remainder by certificates issued by Army quartermasters and commissaries in payment for supplies and by notes given to soldiers for their pay. The Confederation government, because of its financial weakness, was unable even to pay the interest on these obligations.

Taking a highly realistic view of this situation, the New Jersey legislature in 1783 made two momentous decisions: it would not make any further financial contributions to the support of the central government and it would assume responsibility for paying the interest on Continental securities owned by its citizens. Accordingly, an annual tax of $83,358 was levied, and a special type of currency known as "revenue money" was issued in that amount. Each year the "revenue money" would be brought into the treasury through taxes and would then be paid out to the security-holders. By this arrangement the public creditors were assured an income on their investments, and they were, on the whole, well pleased with the arrangement.

In addition to the Continental securities, there were also state debts, totaling about seven hundred fifty thousand dollars and comprising notes issued for militia pay, for payments due to soldiers, and for supplies. Because of the confused nature of the accounts, it was several years before the amount of the indebtedness could be roughly calculated, but by 1787 some degree of order had been instituted and an annual tax of $33,333 was imposed to produce sufficient funds to service the debt.

New Jersey's financial plight was especially grave in that, unlike many states, it had no public lands that could be sold to produce a revenue and no tariff duties. Consequently, an extremely heavy burden of taxes had to be placed on property owners alone. During the decade prior to the inauguration of the new federal government, the citizens of New Jersey paid higher taxes than they were to pay at any time prior to the Civil War in order to meet not only the ordinary costs of the State government but also the interest payments on Continental debts. For obvious reasons the state looked forward to the day when the central government would possess the necessary powers to meet its own financial obligations.

An appraisal of the manner in which the State attempted to cope with the manifold problems of what has been called the "critical period" suggests that these were not years of discord and disintegration but rather years marked by constructive achievements in many areas. By 1787 the major tasks of rehabilitation and reconstruction had been accomplished. The damages, social and material, that were a heritage of the war had been repaired, the postwar economic depression was nearly over, and ingenious methods had been adopted to meet the especially critical currency and debt problems. All was not well, however. New Jersey's relations with the central government were unsatisfactory, and, indeed, its confidence in that government was negligible. What was needed was a new frame of government to replace the Articles of Confederation.

NEW JERSEY AND THE CONFEDERATION

New Jersey had early taken the position that the central government should have more extensive powers than those conferred by the Articles of Confederation. Most particularly it urged that the Continental Congress should be able to regulate trade, levy tariff duties, and control western lands. These views were strongly influenced by financial considerations. If Congress possessed revenues from duties and land sales, it would not have to call upon the state for funds and it would be able to meet its obligations to the public creditors. New Jersey stated its position at length in a "Representation" to Congress on June 16, 1778, when it urged alterations in the proposed Articles. Subsequently, in November, the State reluctantly gave its assent to the nation's first constitution, acknowledging that "every separate and State-Interest ought to be postponed to the public Good."

New Jersey's conviction that the Articles were defective in their fiscal provisions was amply demonstrated. Congress could borrow money without limitation, but it had to rely on "requisitions" on the states (requests for funds on a quota basis) to pay these debts. By 1781 it had become apparent that the requisition system was a failure, and Congress sought from the states power to levy import duties. It could not secure the unanimous consent necessary. Again, in 1783, Congress made a similar effort, with equally frustrating consequences. It was at this point, in December, 1783, that the New Jersey legislature declared that until Congress was vested with the power to collect tariff duties, it would make no further contributions to the support of the Confederation.

Two years later Congress sought to extricate itself from its all but hopeless situation by calling urgently upon the states to pay the amounts requisitioned from them. By this time New Jersey was more obdurate than ever because of its mounting resentment against the tariff policies of New York and Pennsylvania. Because the bulk of its foreign imports were obtained through those states, New Jersey was contributing substantially to the support of its neighbors. It very much preferred that all duties should go to the central government, where they would benefit, in part at least, the citizens of New Jersey. Consequently the legislature in February, 1786, ardently reaffirmed its refusal to honor any requisitions from Congress until other states should "forbear exacting Duties or Imposts upon Goods and Merchandise for the particular Benefit of their respective States, thereby drawing Revenues from other States whose local Situations and Circumstances will not admit their enjoying similar advantages from Commerce."

This defiant action shocked Congress so deeply that it appointed a three-man delegation to appear before the State legislature and make a special plea for the requisition. The emissaries were accorded a respectful hearing, but the legislature would not alter its policy. This incident, coming when it did, dealt the Confederation a severe blow and heightened the general sense of despair about the adequacy of the Articles. Indeed, like Shays' Rebellion, it was one of the major crises that hastened the movement that was to culminate in the Constitutional Convention.

New Jersey was equally obdurate in its insistence that the western lands should belong to the states collectively and should be managed by Congress for the benefit of all. It contended that the region west of the Appalachians had become vested in the Crown in 1763 and that now it belonged rightfully to the nation as a whole rather than to those states—like Virginia, New York, and North Carolina—that laid claim to the area on the basis of their early charters. New Jersey's attitude was obviously conditioned by the fact that it was a "landless" state, with no basis for claims to the West. Moreover, it saw the western lands as an important source of revenue for the central government, and saw that, if they were under the control of Congress, citizens of New Jersey would have equal access to them. The State had set forth its views on this important issue in its "Representation" of 1778, and thereafter it continued to insist that Virginia, together with the other "landed" states, should cede their claims.

Ultimately, of course, the cessions were made, and Congress arranged for the disposal of its vast domain by sales to both individuals and speculative companies. In New Jersey a group of enterprising men, headed by John Cleves Symmes and including such prominent figures as Elias Boudinot, Jonathan Dayton, General Elias Dayton, and Joseph Bloomfield, entered into negotiations with Congress in 1787 and purchased a large tract in southwestern Ohio along the Great Miami River.

Symmes, a former legislator, supreme court justice,

and delegate to Congress, was appointed one of the first three judges of the Northwest Territory. He and his associates advertised widely to attract prospective settlers, and in July, 1788, Symmes set forth from Morristown at the head of a caravan of Ohio-bound emigrants. Although the venture was plagued with financial difficulties and controversies over the boundaries of the Miami Purchase, it led in due course to the founding of Cincinnati, the naming of the city of Dayton, and a strong New Jersey influence in that portion of Ohio. Other groups were formed in the State for the purpose of obtaining similar tracts in the western territory, but they came to naught. Nevertheless, hundreds of individuals joined the trek to the new lands that had been secured to the nation in conformity with the foresighted policy so vigorously pressed by New Jersey.

New Jersey's attitude toward the Confederation was strongly influenced by the hope, and even the expectation, that it might provide the site for the permanent capital of the new nation. Even before the Continental Congress fled from the tumult of Philadelphia to the rural tranquillity of Princeton in June, 1783, the legislature had offered to cede twenty square miles of land and donate £30,000 for such a purpose. While Congress was at Princeton, it deliberated on the matter of the proper location for a capital, and late in October, after considerable inter-sectional intrigue, it voted to build *two* capitals, one on the Delaware and the other on the Potomac. Pending the construction of the new facilities, Congress was to meet alternately at Annapolis and Trenton.

After leaving Princeton, the delegates held a brief session at Annapolis and then prepared to convene next at Trenton on October 30, 1784. In anticipation of their arrival, the legislature appropriated funds to be used in refurbishing Jacob Bergen's French Arms Tavern as a meeting place for Congress and for renovating the house of Stacy Potts as a residence for the president of Congress. Once on the scene, the Congressmen looked forward to an early removal, for they found that desirable accommodations were scarce because the State legislature was also in session in the small town. Before departing, however, they resolved that there should be only *one* federal city and that it should be located at the falls of the Delaware, near Trenton. After appointing commissioners to select the exact site and appropriating $100,-000 for the erection of buildings, they moved on to New York City, which had been designated as the temporary capital.

At this point New Jersey's hopes were justifiably high. But no funds were actually made available to the commissioners, and the whole capital question remained in abeyance until after the ratification of the Constitution. On the recommendation of the State ratifying convention, the legislature offered to cede a ten-mile square for a Federal district. Meanwhile the Continental Congress in one of its last actions decided that the first session of the new Federal Congress should be held in New York. New Jersey continued to assume that in accordance with the decision reached at Trenton in 1784, the capital would ultimately be located near the falls of the Delaware. Fate, and the machinations of Alexander Hamilton, decreed otherwise. It is now well known that in order to secure southern support for his plan for the assumption of state debts, Hamilton arranged a bargain that resulted in the location of the capital on the Potomac. Thus Washington, rather than Trenton, became the nation's capital.

NEW JERSEY AND THE FEDERAL CONSTITUTION

Because of its long standing conviction that the Articles of Confederation were defective in many particulars, New Jersey played a leading role in the movement that eventuated in the adoption of a new constitution. All interest groups—debtors and creditors, paper-money advocates and champions of hard-money, farmers and merchants, bankrupts and security-holders —saw the obvious advantages to be derived from a central government possessed of adequate powers to meet its financial obligations. Conservatives had in mind placing some limitations on the powers of the democratically controlled state legislature, especially where the rights of property were involved. Not least among the contributing factors was the general feeling that unless something was done to strengthen the Union, the promising experiments in republicanism and independence for which thousands of Jerseymen had made great sacrifices, would end in failure.

The call for a constitutional convention grew out of the Annapolis Convention, to which the Virginia legislature invited all the state to send delegates for the purpose of considering an extension of Congress' power over trade. New Jersey responded promptly to the invitation and gave very broad instructions to its three delegates: Abraham Clark, William Churchill Houston, and James Schureman. The legislature authorized its Commissioners to discuss not only trade regulations, but also "other important Matters" in order that the Articles might be so revised as to be adequate to "the Exigencies of the Union."

The Convention was not well attended, and those who were present decided that under the circumstances it would be fruitless to pursue their original purpose. Instead, they recommended that a second convention should be held. In their report they expressed the opinion "that the Idea of extending the power of their deputies to other objects than those of Commerce, which has been adopted by the State of New Jersey, was an improvement on the original plan, and will deserve to be incorporated into that of a future Convention." Accordingly, they proposed that a convention should be held in May, 1787, in Philadelphia to "render the constitution of the Federal Government adequate to the exigencies of the Union." Thus the "New Jersey Idea" provided the bridge between Annapolis and Philadelphia.

New Jersey was the first state to appoint delegates to the Philadelphia convention, acting even before the Continental Congress had given its endorsement to the meeting. The five men who ultimately made up the State's delegation were all well-tested patriots. William

Livingston, the venerable governor of the State, went to Philadelphia inspired by the hope that the new nation he loved so deeply would be rescued from the perils that beset it. David Brearly had been an officer in the State militia before becoming the chief justice of the State supreme court in 1779 and subsequently became a Federal district court judge. The most influential member of the delegation was William Paterson. A graduate of Princeton, he had been the wartime attorney-general of the State and later achieved eminence as governor, as a United States Senator, and an associate justice of the Supreme Court. Jonathan Dayton was, at twenty-seven, the youngest member of the Federal Convention. He had fought as a captain in the Continental Army and was to become speaker of the House of Representatives and a United States Senator before being forced into political oblivion because of his implication in the Burr scandal. William Churchill Houston, who was obliged to leave the Convention because of ill health after a week of attendance, was an able lawyer and former member of the Continental Congress.

The delegation, and especially Paterson, played a leading role in the controversy that threatened for several weeks to disrupt the convention. The Virginia delegation had proposed a plan of government that would have accorded the states representation on a basis of population. The small states disliked this arrangement and put forward what became known as the "New Jersey Plan," which gave each state equal representation. Ultimately, the conflict was resolved by the "Great Compromise," whereby each state was given equal weight in the Senate, while the House of Representatives was apportioned according to population. Paterson, the leading architect of the "New Jersey Plan," readily acquiesced in this solution, as did his colleagues. Where matters involving the powers of the new central government were concerned, New Jersey in accordance with its frequently reiterated views, was disposed to give wide latitude to the Congress.

When at last the Convention had finished its delibera-

William Paterson

A strong Whig, Paterson served as secretary of the first Provincial Congress, as war-time attorney general, and as a prominent member of the Constitutional Convention. Subsequently he filled the offices of governor, United States Senator, and Justice of the United States Supreme Court.

tions and published its handiwork late in September, 1787, the immediate reaction in New Jersey was overwhelmingly favorable. Recognizing this preponderant sentiment, the legislature when it convened in October was unanimous in providing promptly for the holding of an election to choose members of a ratifying convention. The voters of the State were to go to the polls on the first Tuesday in November and elect three men from each county to convene in Trenton on the first Tuesday in December. Judging from the meager contemporary reports, the election went off quietly, with no signs of opposition anywhere.

The delegates who assembled at Francis Witt's Blazing Star Tavern on December 11 were almost without exception "early Whigs" who had held either civil or military offices during the Revolution. Most of them were farmers, with a sprinkling of lawyers, doctors, merchants, and ministers and the presidents of the State's two colleges. The President of the Convention was John Stevens, one of the wealthiest men in the State, who had begun his political career as a member of the Assembly in 1751 and had later served on the governor's council and in the State legislature. Also in attendance was Chief Justice Brearly, whose participation in the Philadelphia Convention gave his views great weight.

After having spent two days in organization, the delegates then devoted three days to a section-by-section discussion of the proposed constitution. According to the sole newspaper report, "many supposed exceptions were agitated," but Brearly, "with a perspicuity of argument and persuasive eloquence, which carried conviction with it, bore down all opposition." On Tuesday, December 18, the vote was taken on ratification and was "determined in the Affirmative unanimously." The next day, after signing the ratification document, the delegates marched in solemn procession from the Blazing Star to the courthouse, where the welcome news was proclaimed to the assembled citizenry that New Jersey had become the third state—following Delaware and Pennsylvania —to ratify the Federal Constitution.

During the ensuing months the people of the State anxiously watched the progress of ratification elsewhere. When at last New Hampshire became the ninth state to ratify, thus assuring the adoption of the new frame of government, there was general rejoicing. The venerable Governor Livingston, who earlier had despaired of the future of the republic, now looked forward with confidence. "We are now arrived at that auspicious Era, which, I confess, I have most earnestly wished to see," he told the legislature. "Thanks to God that I have lived to see it."

Now it only remained to place the new government in operation. The legislature in November, 1788, arranged for elections to be held to choose the various officials authorized by the new Constitution. To the governor and his privy council was entrusted the responsibility for naming six electors, who in due course voted unanimously for Washington for president. The legislature, meeting once again in Nassau Hall, elected William Paterson and Jonathan Elmer, a Cumberland County physician who had served in the Continental Congress, to the United States Senate. Four congressmen were chosen from the state-at-large in an election that began in February and, marked by incredible frauds, continued for several weeks. When the first Federal Congress assembled, it was presented with its first case of a disputed election as a result of the irregularities that had marred the New Jersey contest, although ultimately the declared winners retained their seats.

Meanwhile, a change had taken place in the political climate within the State. Heartened by the adoption of the Constitution, the conservative forces had gained ascendancy, and they proceeded to reverse the radicalism that had marked the "paper money" era. Measures were enacted to hasten the retirement from circulation of the "revenue money" and the loan-office bills; the laws that had been passed to favor debtors were repealed; the restrictions that had long been imposed on Tories were lifted; and Perth Amboy and Burlington, both strongholds of conservatism and Toryism, were once again designated the twin capitals of the state. It was this conservative alliance, too, that backed the four candidates—Elias Boudinot, Lambert Cadwalader, James Schureman, and Thomas Sinnickson—whose election produced so much discord. Stanchly federalist in outlook, the new political leadership of the State was determined to insure to New Jersey the stability promised by the Constitution.

In retrospect, it would seem that the moment for which the people of New Jersey—and indeed of all the states—had been preparing themselves for many decades had at last arrived. Starting from the humblest origins, a new society had taken form in the English colonies. It was a remarkably free and capable society, basically demoratic in its social, economic, and political institutions. But with its strong commitment to private property, individual rights, and limitations on the role of government, it was an orderly society.

By the time the decision for independence had been reached, sound experience had been acquired in the ways of self-government and there was a growing sense of national identity. The common sacrifices in the Revolution tested the new society's qualities for survival and heightened the feeling of national unity. And now, held together despite the inadequacies of the Articles of Confederation and the difficulties of the postwar era, the states had devised a novel and promising solution to the problem of Union. New Jersey's evolution from a Colony to a State was representative of the common experience; its contributions to the building of the new nation were at least commensurate with its size and resources; it could take its place proudly among the United States of America.

BIBLIOGRAPHICAL NOTE

There are rich collections of printed source materials for the period covered by this study. Of outstanding importance are the *New Jersey Archives,* 1st series, I-XXX, and 2nd series, I-V, published by The New Jersey Historical Society, 1880-1917. Indispensable for the proprietary period are Aaron Leaming and Jacob Spicer, *The Grants, Concessions, and Original Constitutions of the Province of New Jersey* (2nd ed.; Somerville, 1891) and *The Journal of the Procedure of the Governor and Council of the Province of East New Jersey* (Newark, 1848). For the Revolutionary era the *Minutes of the Provincial Congress and the Council of Safety of the State of New Jersey* (Trenton, 1879) and *Selections from the Correspondence of the Executive of New Jersey, from 1776 to 1786* (Newark, 1848) are most useful. A remarkable work, still worthy of study, is Samuel Smith, *The History of the Colony of Nova-Caesaria, or New Jersey* (Burlington, 1765). *The Collections* (12 vols.; 1847-1959) and the *Proceedings* (81 vols.; Newark, 1846-1963) of The New Jersey Historical Society contain a wealth of material on every aspect of New Jersey history.

For the years before New Jersey became a royal colony, the two most serviceable studies are John E. Pomfret's *The Province of West New Jersey, 1609-1702* (Princeton, 1956) and his companion work, *The Province of East New Jersey, 1609-1702* (Princeton, 1962). Dorothy Cross, *The Indians of New Jersey* (Trenton, 1955) is a brief but authoritative treatment, which can be supplemented by Daniel G. Brinton, *The Lenape and their Legends* (Philadelphia, 1885). Excellent contemporary accounts of early exploration and settlement may be found in John Franklin Jameson (ed.), *Narratives of New Netherland, 1609-1664* (New York, 1909) and Albert Cook Myers (ed.),

Narratives of Early Pennsylvania, West New Jersey and Delaware, 1630-1707 (New York, 1912). Amandus Johnson, *The Swedish Settlements on the Delaware* (2 vols.; New York, 1911) is definitive in its field. There is as yet no adequate treatment of the Dutch in New Jersey, but Charles H. Winfield, *History of the County of Hudson, New Jersey* (New York, 1874) is relevant. A succinct account of the early proprietorship by a brilliant scholar will be found in the third volume of Charles McLean Andrews, *The Colonial Period of American History* (New Haven, 1937). Not to be neglected are William A. Whitehead's early, but still rewarding, *East Jersey under the Proprietary Governments* (2nd ed.; Newark, 1875); Edwin A. Hatfield, *History of Elizabeth, New Jersey* (New York, 1868); and the historical Introduction in H. Clay Reed and George J. Miller, *The Burlington Court Book . . . 1680-1709* (Washington, D.C., 1944).

Several excellent monographs treat of the history of New Jersey between 1702 and 1776. The most comprehensive is Donald L. Kemmerer, *Path to Freedom* (Princeton, 1940), but additional detail on political and institutional developments will be found in Edwin P. Tanner, *The Province of New Jersey, 1664-1738* (New York, 1908) and Edgar J. Fisher, *New Jersey as a Royal Province, 1738-1776* (New York, 1911). Of value for the treatment of special topics are Nelson R. Burr, *Education in New Jersey, 1630-1871* (Princeton, 1942); Charles S. Boyer, *Early Forges and Furnaces in New Jersey* (Philadelphia, 1931); Wheaton J. Lane, *From Indian Trail to Iron Horse* (Princeton, 1939); Richard P. McCormick, *The History of Voting in New Jersey* (New Brunswick, 1953); Thomas Jefferson Wertenbaker, *The Founding of American Civilization: the Middle Colonies* (New York, 1938); and Carl R. Woodward, *Ploughs and Politics* (New Brunswick, 1941).

There is a vast bibliography on New Jersey's participation in the Revolution. The standard work is Leonard Lundin, *Cockpit of the Revolution* (Princeton, 1940). For tracing the course of military events, volumes four and five of Douglas Southall Freeman's masterly *George*

Washington, a Biography (New York, 1951-1952) are invaluable. Outstanding special studies are Alfred Hoyt Bill, *The Campaign of Princeton, 1776-1777* (Princeton, 1948); Charles R. Erdman, *The New Jersey Constitution of 1776* (Princeton, 1929); Adrian C. Leiby, *The Revolutionary War in the Hackensack Valley* (New Brunswick, 1962); and William S. Stryker, *The Battle of Monmouth,* edited by William Starr Myers (Princeton, 1927). A thoroughly delightful account of the Revolution in the Raritan Valley is Andrew D. Mellick, Jr., *The Story of an Old Farm* (Somerville, 1889), republished, with an introduction by Hubert G. Schmidt, as *Lesser Crossroads* (New Brunswick, 1948).

Among the more important biographies are George Adams Boyd's excellent *Elias Boudinot, Patriot and Statesman, 1740-1821* (Princeton, 1952); Gertrude S. Wood, *William Paterson of New Jersey, 1745-1806* (Fair Lawn, 1933); and the lamentably inadequate Theodore Sedgwick, *A Memoir of the Life of William Livingston* (New York, 1833). For the Confederation period the standard work is Richard P. McCormick, *Experiment in Independence: New Jersey in the Critical Period, 1781-1789* (New Brunswick, 1950).

BRIEF HISTORICAL CHRONOLOGY
OF NEW JERSEY
1609-1787

1609—Henry Hudson's voyage of exploration.

1629—Beginnings of Dutch settlement at Pavonia (Jersey City).

1638—Sweden established colony on lower Delaware.

1655—Dutch conquest of Swedish colony.

1664—English conquest of New Netherland; grant of New Jersey by Duke of York to Berkeley and Carteret.

1665-7—Founding of Elizabethtown, Middletown, Shrewsbury, Woodbridge, Piscataway and Newark.

1674—Sale of Berkeley's half interest in New Jersey to Quakers.

1676—Quintipartite deed established dividing line between East and West Jersey.

1681—East Jersey acquired by the "Twenty-four Proprietors."

1688-92—New Jersey absorbed in Dominion of New England.

1702—Proprietors of East and West Jersey surrendered their powers of government to Crown.

1703—East and West Jersey united under royal governor.

1738—New Jersey received own royal governor; no longer shared with New York.

1743—John Lawrence surveyed dividing line.

1745—Beginnings of decade of land riots.

1746—Founding of College of New Jersey (Princeton University).

1758—Establishment of Indian reservation at Brotherton.

1765—Protests against Stamp Act; Sons of Liberty.

1766—Chartering of Queen's College (Rutgers, the State University).
1769—Decision on boundary between New York and New Jersey.
1774—Organization of Committees of Correspondence.
1775—Meeting of first Provincial Congress.
1776—First state constitution; William Livingston first governor; Battle of Trenton.
1777—Battle of Princeton; Washington's first winter encampment at Morristown.
1778-9—Battle of Monmouth; Washington's encampment at Middlebrook (Bound Brook).
1779-80—Washington's second encampment at Morristown; Battle of Springfield.
1783—Continental Congress at Princeton.
1784—Continental Congress at Trenton.
1786—New Jersey delegates participated in Annapolis Convention.
1787—New Jersey the third state to ratify the Federal Constitution.

INDEX

10; humanitarian concern for, 102-103; removal of, from state, 103
Ingoldsby, Gov. Richard: 67
Inian, John: 85
Iron industry: 89-91, 162

James, Duke of York: 16, 17-18, 35, 39, 44
Jennings, Samuel: 46ff., 49, 66
Jersey, Island of, 18
Jersey City: 11
Jockey Hollow: 148
Johnstone, Dr. John: 68
Judicial system: 62, 124

Keith, George: 52
Keith Line: 76
Kemble, Peter: 127
King's Highway: 86
Kingston: 143
Kinsey, James: 114
Kinsey, John, Jr.: 68
Knox, Gen. Henry: 139, 148

Lafayette, Marquis de: 146
Lambertville: 85, 146
Land riots: 70, 77-78
Land system: basis of, in East Jersey, 18-21, 25-26, 28, 29; changes in, 32-33; controversies over, in proprietary period, 19, 26-29, 33, 35; basis of, in West Jersey, 40-41, 44-45, 48, 55-56; and political controversies, 64-67; riots over, 70, 77-78
Lawrence, John: 76, 127
Lawrence's Line: 77
Lawrie, Gawen: 39, 40
Lawrie's Road: 85
Lee, Gen. Charles: 137, 147
Lenni Lenape: *see* Indians

Leslie, Gen. Alexander: 141
Lincoln, Gen. John: 144
Literature: 101-102
Little Egg Harbor: 27, 76, 151
Livingston, Rev. John: 94
Livingston, Gov. William: 84, 114, 123, 126, 129, 134 153, 160, 171, 174; portrait of, *125*
Loantaka Valley: 144
Long Pond: 90
Lovelace, John, Lord: 67
Loyalists: appearance of, 118, 121; characterizations of, 127-128; sufferings of, 128; during British invasion, 138; activities of, 151-153; departure of, 154; end of restrictions on, 174
Lucas, Nicholas: 39, 40
Lyon, James: 101

Matawan: 8
Maurice River: 83
Mawhood, Col. Charles: 142
Maxwell, Gen. William: 117, 133
Mays Landing: 8, 151
McKonkey's Ferry: 138
Medford: 8
Medical Society, New Jersey: 100, 160
Melfort, Earl of: 31
Mercer, Gen. Hugh: 133, 139
Methodist Church: 95
Metuchen: 8, 145
Miami Purchase: 167-168
Middlebrook, 144, 145, 148
Middlesex County: 34, 77, 82, 127, 154
Middletown: 21, 29, 30, 94
Mifflin, Gen. Thomas: 141
Militia system: 116-117, 132-134